REDISCOVERING HOLINESS

Rediscovering Holiness

MELVYN MATTHEWS

First published 1996 in Great Britain
The Society for Promoting Christian Knowledge
Holy Trinity Church
Marylebone Road
London
NW1 4DU

British Library Cataloguing in Publication Data
A catalogue record for this book is available from the British
Library.
ISBN 0-281-04914-9

Typeset by Datix International Limited, Bungay, Suffolk
Printed in Great Britain by Biddles Ltd., Guildford and King's Lynn

Contents

Acknowledgements

This book first came into being as a series of lectures which I delivered in Wells Cathedral during Lent 1994 under the title 'The Quest for Holiness Today'. I have rewritten the original lectures quite substantially in preparation for this book as the spoken word is never the same as the text on the page. I would like to record my gratitude to 'Theology in Wells' for the invitation to give the lectures and to Canon George Farran, Chancellor of Wells, and his wife Pamela for their kindness and hospitality to me and my wife while the lectures were being delivered. I am also grateful to Ian Thompson and his friends for producing transcripts of the lectures at the time. A form of the chapter on Monastic Holiness was first published in the *Merton Journal* (May 1994) under the title 'The Monastic Way'. I am grateful to the editor for permission to include it, albeit somewhat rewritten, in this book.

Foreword

One of the most important insights of this book comes at the very end, where Melvyn Matthews warns that 'Even prayer can become an item on the consumerist shopping list'. We need to read the pages that follow with that in mind, read them against the background of a consumerized and trivialized understanding of spirituality. These are hard and threatening times nationally, internationally and, for many people, personally as well; the temptation to turn to 'spiritual values' or to some sort of esoteric religious practice that promises release from anxiety is a powerful one, and thus a very marketable proposition. The trouble is that it means reconceiving the life of the spirit in terms of what the market requires: which is a poor recipe for transformation or for prophecy.

Melvyn Matthews has quarried both traditional and contemporary sources to evoke the possibility of a religious sensibility that is centrally and essentially a way of perceiving and living in the world; a training in apprehending the ordinary as extraordinary. From such a training – which involves learning to read the biblical story as our own, so that we *participate* in the action of God with human beings whose pattern Scripture lays out before us – we learn to live with alertness or (to borrow the Buddhist term) mindfulness in the world. Our *commitment* to the world is deepened, not diminished, by the capacity to live with detachment – that is, to live in the world in a way that does not constantly order the world around the pivotal points of my needs and my reactions. And if we can grow into commitment like this, our action for justice in society will be significantly different – capable of living with incompleteness and limitation, with an ambiguous world where solutions are not always to be had and never to be had swiftly and innocently; capable of living with silence, with something of the patience of Jesus, while living also with the *passion* of Jesus for the healing of the world.

One recent writer on spirituality[1] points out where the missing link so often is in our thinking about this subject: we are often prone, he says, to come to our religious or 'spiritual' practice with the same chaotic and selfish emotions we bring to our usual transactions and relations. Spiritual growth means acquiring something like new emotions. Melvyn Matthews' concern with reconstructing our ways of seeing and experiencing looks in the same direction. This is the opposite of a consumerized spirituality, just as much as it is the enemy of an obsession with 'interiority' for its own sake or a purely psychological attempt at self-discovery or self-realization. Here is a readable, practical book, accessible to any thoughtful reader, Christian or not, which puts before us a challenge that is deeply radical but in no way shrill or manipulative. It is a challenge to rediscover some fundamental human *skills*, skills of being, skills of simplicity.

+ ROWAN WILLIAMS

[1] Jacob Needleman, *Lost Christianity* (New York 1980).

Prologue

FIRST OF ALL let me spend one or two moments saying why I have chosen to write about 'Rediscovering Holiness'. The first reason should be very clear – I believe that we need, more than ever before, a holy Church. We live in deeply disturbing and challenging times, times when all is in flux, when much that was apparently true and settled turns out not to be so. I believe that in these days Christian people are called to live out the gospel in a way which requires much dedication, much prayer and enormous openness to the work of God in their lives. This situation is not new. Whenever there has been flux and change, the Church has responded by throwing up people or movements which live the essence of the gospel life. At the time of Constantine the Desert Fathers moved away from the centres of urbanization and tried to discover what the essence of a faithful life really was. St Benedict took up the same challenge when the Roman Empire lost its sway over Europe. Later on St Francis and St Dominic found new ways to speak about faith and to live faithfully within the wealthy and urbanized élite of the great cities. I believe that today we need a similar search for and loyalty to the essence of Christian faith if we are to come through the present disintegration with any real Church at all. But above all such a search must be for a form of 'being Christian' which is appropriate to our own age and both understands and challenges the spirit of that age.

Related to this is the situation of the Church itself. Over the last twenty-five years, since my ordination, we have devoted ourselves to massive and long-needed reform. We now have liturgies in the language of the people, we have genuinely synodical government, we have equality and security in the pay and housing of the clergy and we have, thankfully, the ordination of women as priests – all long-needed structural reforms to the Church which have taken up our energies for twenty-five years or more. There is still more to do; but we will not, I believe, progress any further now unless we also make progress in the evangelical life. It is no good having properly paid, democratically in-clined clergy if none of them can pray. It is no use having systems of collaborative ministry between clergy and laity if nobody asks what are we trying to achieve by means of these schemes. We have now to return to that inner search for God. Issues of ministry and management must be tackled by a holy Church.

I also believe that such a search is part of the Decade of Evangelism. I have very serious doubts about many church growth strategies, church planting and the theology which accompanies such policies. Much of this seems to me to be no more than a form of spiritual materialism, a packaging of the Church in the spirit of the age. I prefer to believe that the conversion of one person to standing still in prayer more often, and the development of a thoughtful and reflective Church, whose worship rests on and derives from a deep sense of the mystery of God, will be more deeply attractive to the people of our age than a Church which, once people have joined it, simply replaces the frenzy of getting and spending of material things with a frenzy of getting and spending in spiritual things. The evidence is that many young people feel starved of a sense of the mystery of God in their lives and are deeply critical of a Church which, while it should be the guardian of this mystery, has frittered it away in an urbane, slick conservative theology and an over-active Church with a facile 'corporate image'. Why else do so many flock to places like Taizé where they are met with nothing more than community life, silence, rich music and icons? Activism in church life is often no more than a blind obedience to the spirit of the age. We need more attention to mystery.

But this search for holiness also poses difficulties and dangers. Even the very act of writing about holiness contains within it an implicit danger. This is because holiness is not something which knows itself. Once holiness knows itself then it ceases to be holiness because it has become self-regarding. 'Those who speak, do not know; those who know, do not speak . . .' This emphasis on the silence or the secrecy of holiness will be a recurrent theme in this book. This is because true holiness does contain within itself a type of self-disregard, a lack of self-awareness, even in some cases, a self-forgetfulness which verges on the extreme – a form of madness for God. What it does not do is continually check itself out, or measure itself against a scale of holiness or another holiness that is somehow regarded as 'the best'. As soon as the soul begins to worry about whether or not it is on the right path to holiness then the risk of losing the path becomes very high. 'When you have found the way, you may have lost God.' All this became very apparent to me when I was the director of an ecumenical conference centre running a number of retreats. I became very disturbed at the self-regarding nature of so many of the people who came, particularly those who were influenced by New Age thinking as well as many within the Christian retreat movement.

So why have I run the risk by writing about the quest for holiness in today's world if, by that very act, I might destroy what I have set out to achieve? Part of the answer is provided by the author of the quotation I have just used – 'If you find the way, you may lose God'. This is a sentence from Meister Eckhart, the German mystic and teacher, who lived in the latter half of the thirteenth century and spent a great deal of his time working with enthusiastic women in the religious communities of the day. Much of this 'enthusiasm' Eckhart found very difficult. He was concerned to find a true way in an age which had gone overboard on religious experience. Without wishing to claim any affinity with Eckhart himself, I think we do live in a similar religious climate. Courses on 'spirituality' proliferate and 'spiritual direction' is a growth industry. It seems that every person you come across is part of one spirituality network or another, or has been, or is going, on a course about it. We are part of a Church which has embraced religious experience with massive enthusiasm – whether this is pentecostal experience, the more private and individual experience of a retreat, or a course in spirituality. This phenomenon needs to be understood and placed in context. Looking at our place within this phenomenon will enable us to see more clearly where we are. For it is not necessarily a good thing in itself. It verges on the anti-intellectual and narcissistic. Eckhart, who found himself in deep trouble with the ecclesiastical authorities of his day (which were, interestingly enough, like much of today's spirituality, Franciscan dominated) because of his attempts to clarify the place of God in the religious life and to distinguish the reality of God from mere religious experience, did at least attempt the task. I feel very strongly that the same needs to be done now.

There is also some theology in all this. God cannot be reduced to our own attempts to experience him. Nor is he 'a spiritual reality'. God is not a spiritual reality whom we can possess or 'get' if we are spiritually gifted. God is not 'a reality' or 'a thing' at all. He simply is and is known by us as whole beings and not known by us through some 'spiritual' sense which is like touch or hearing. This might seem a surprising thing to say, but it is not my own thought. Herbert McCabe, the Roman Catholic Dominican theologian, says, 'God cannot be a thing, an existent among others. It is not possible that God and the Universe should add up to make two.'[1] So the growth of enthusiasm for religious experience risks making a category mistake in understanding God, thus reducing the reality of God to the level of another thing, this time a 'spiritual' thing which you can know or which operates like other things, only 'spiritually'.

But I also think that we need to look carefully at the growth of spirituality in our day because of the way it risks a disconnectedness with this world. Not long after I became the director of the retreat and conference centre I mentioned earlier, I wrote an article in the Roman Catholic journal *The Tablet* called 'The Director's Dilemma', which caused quite a little storm at the time. In this article I puzzled over the question as to why people apparently valued courses on 'spirituality' more highly than courses on the quest for peace and justice in a violent world. I arranged weekend conferences on 'Reconciliation' – which God only knows is the thing we need – but even when they figured people from Corrymeela or similar places dedicated to reconciliation and peace, these weekends never recruited enough participants. On the other hand, weekends on 'Celtic Mysticism' or 'New Age Spirituality' never failed. I wrote then (and some years later I would say the same, even more strongly),

A spirituality which remains self-regarding cannot claim to be a genuine spirituality . . . From the joy of discovering prayer and the consequent awareness this discovery brings of personal wholeness . . . there must emerge a profound moral concern for the whole of creation.

This, then, is a further reason why it is important to risk talking about holiness – to find a way of being holy in today's world which releases that profound moral concern.

To put it simply, I believe that much talk about holiness or spirituality is cheap talk. It is talk which makes a category mistake about God, talk which misses the whole dimension of a renewed moral life, talk which misses what St Benedict calls the conversion of manners. Holiness which claims to be so but which lacks a concern for peace and justice in the world is deficient.

The other thing I want to do at the beginning of this book is to issue a strong government health warning. In these pages I shall talk a good deal about prayer, spirituality, holiness and so on and shall emphasize the importance of a recovery of the mystical sense. Much of what I say has been influenced by Thomas Merton – the great American mystic. But, whatever I might say about mysticism or holiness, nothing of what I say should be taken to imply that the regular, normal practices of the Christian way can be abandoned. There is no special or extra-curricular way to holiness for special extra-curricular people. We all have to go through the normal processes. There is no new way in a New Age – and I use that language very advisedly. There is no new way in a New Age which abandons regular private prayer, regular frequent communion, attendance at church, sitting on church councils, going to synods or cold cathedrals, and praying with people whom you do not particularly like. If anything, the discovery of the presence of God in your lives and growth in holiness will drive you back to these things. Part of the way of holiness in our day is the discovery that God is known in all things and not, particularly, in special experiences. Holy people are those who are, quite simply, aware of that truth and who live it without fuss or difficulty.

A similar health warning occurs in two quite different places in the Christian tradition. The first is in the prologue to *The Cloud of Unknowing*, that treatise on the Christian life which was written sometime in the fourteenth century, where the author warns that nobody should read the book, or pass it to somebody else, unless they are determined to be a perfect follower of Christ, and that in the active life as well as in the contemplative life. The ideal reader, he says, will be he 'who is doing all that he can, and has been presumably for a long time past, to fit himself for the contemplative life by the virtues and exercises of the active life'. In our case, this means, I believe, attending church meetings or being a good Christian teacher or pursuing your vocation actively in the world where you are and doing all this joyfully.

The other warning comes from a better known source: C. S. Lewis. In *The Screwtape Letters*, Lewis has the Senior Devil urge his junior counterpart to tempt his newly fledged Christian with thoughts of higher and better experiences. Then he will begin to scorn the church he prays in and the fat butcher that he has to sit next to every Sunday! The point does not need expanding.

But enough of these warnings and preliminary remarks. Let me give you a brief overview of what this book is about. What I want to do is to look at a number of different contemporary 'ways of holiness'. These are all different quests for a central, co-ordinating way of seeing things which are coming into prominence in different parts of the Christian churches in the present era.

They are:

1. The contemporary resurgence of interest in monastic or quasi-monastic paths. Much of this is to be found in France and Europe.
2. The resurgence of interest in scriptural spirituality

    – much of which is associated with Roman Catholic women writers.

3. The growth of interest in mystical awareness – the Alister Hardy research unit showing us that this is far more widespread than previously thought.
4. Social and evangelical holiness movements, some of which are influenced by liberation theology, others by scriptural study.
5. An overall look in which I shall make some wider comments and suggestions of my own.

In each case, I want not just to talk about these movements but also to see whether they are of this age only or whether they are genuinely a development of the tradition in which we stand.

But there is, behind all of this, a sub-text, an inner theme – which is perhaps why this book is called *Rediscovering Holiness*. It has become clear to all of us that the institutional Christian Church in Western Europe is in a state of decline. I believe that we can recover our confidence, turn away from our loss of nerve, not so much through attempts to build up our numbers, nor through attempts to build up our doctrine, though restatements of traditional doctrines are needed. I regard these as secondary unless we also recover an interior sense of God's grace and so an interior life where God in Christ is known. Nor do I mean by this phrase 'interior life' an emotional life – although emotions are naturally involved. I mean a deep sense that our beings are open to God and can be translucent to God. Interior sacramental holiness, or interior sacramental awareness, is perhaps a better phrase. Once we have refound this, then I believe that the Church will recover in the shape and form that it needs to recover in the twentieth century – which is not necessarily the shape and form that contemporary ecclesiastical managers or evangelical enthusiasts sometimes want to give it. I believe that this interior sacramental awareness or the transparency of our being towards God will work and should be left to do its own work for the Church. Recovering this sense of translucency before God is the recovery of the Church as a whole. The world will change because of it and whatever changes are put in hand without it will only need to be changed again when we have found it.

So this book is called *Rediscovering Holiness* because I believe there has been so much in modern life which has caused this sense of translucency of the spirit to disappear and it is the task of the churches to refind it. Strangely enough I do not think that it is war or the violence of our age which has caused this disappearance, as if the mere cessation of violence will cause it to resurface. I believe the root of this disappearance lies further back in the individualism and materialism of the twentieth century which itself derives from over-confidence in rationalism (and I stress over-confidence, for there is a proper confidence that we need to have in reason) which was generated during the eighteenth century.

So we need to recover our inner transparency towards God. And I think that this is often better done by a number of apparently 'secular' agencies – such as poets, novelists, those involved in therapy and counselling (especially those in the Jungian tradition) and by scientific investigation, which itself needs an openness to the unknown to function properly – rather than by

some sections of the Church with their vastly diminished sense of the unknown, the banality of much of
their music and their preoccupation with 'mission',
which is almost another word for 'progress' or 'market-
ing' and so infinitely suspect.

One of these poets is R. S. Thomas. He says,

> He is that great void
> we must enter, calling
> to one another on our way
> . . .
> Enough we have been given wings
> and a needle in the mind
> to respond to his bleak north.[2]

So let us see where that needle is pointing in our
present age.

ONE

Monastic Holiness

SEVERAL SUMMERS AGO my wife and I visited the monastery and monastic community of St Benoit-sur-Loire in France. We toured the monastery on Saturday and returned for Mass on Sunday. It is the most lovely Romanesque building, simple but glowing with light. The coloured Roman pavement under the nave altar is quite stunning. At the Mass the church was full and afterwards we lingered in the bookshop which was full of books on prayer and the spiritual life together with a great deal on the Bible, which is the subject of renewed interest by French Catholics amongst others.

So it was a warm, active and reflective community which welcomed us. The sermon during the Mass was a very intelligent exposition of a modern position on market economics – critical of capitalism, but affirming of the need for wealth creation. It reminded me of a number of similar recent statements by the Anglican Bishop of Oxford. Moreover, the liturgy was very Anglican, with lay participation and a degree of style but no frills, so I felt quite at home. The community there is, like all French monastic communities, a renewed one, dating from this century. It was obviously attractive to the young people of the modern age, for many were there. It is a community that is not only prayerful but also intellectually rigorous and socially committed. I came away, and not for the first time, deeply impressed by the vigour and thoughtfulness of this strand of French Catholic life. Much current Anglicanism, either management obsessed or emotionally obsessed, running scared in the face of lack of numbers, is quite simply flabby by comparison.

I have described this community at length because it struck me as being one of the best examples of what somebody has called 'a new form of community within which the moral life could be sustained so that both morality and civility might survive the coming barbarism and darkness'.[1] In other words it is a community within which a life of praise and prayer is linked with communal love and a common intellectual reflection to preserve a fully moral life of openness to God – and by moral I do not mean simply 'behaving correctly', but also behaving with love and thoughtfulness stemming from prayer and praise and work. No wonder it was full up and crowded with visitors.

The interesting thing is that that quotation, about the need for new forms of community within which the moral life can be sustained, comes from the end of an important book called *After Virtue* by the Scottish Catholic philosopher, Alasdair MacIntyre. I was reminded of the quotation while I was at St Benoit-sur-Loire because the monastery houses the remains of St Benedict himself. We visited the crypt and paid our respects. The legend is that St Benoit-sur-Loire had been founded by monks from St Benedict's own community in Italy very early on, but later they heard that St Benedict had been killed as the country was invaded from the north and so they sent out a small search party and recovered his remains and brought them back to France.

This reminded me of MacIntyre's book because at the end he calls for a new St Benedict in our day. He says, 'We are waiting not for a Godot, but for another – doubtless very different – St Benedict.' MacIntyre considers that Western civilization is at a crisis point markedly similar to that which obtained at the end of the Roman Empire. Then, he says,

> Men and women of goodwill turned aside from the task of shoring up the Roman *imperium* and ceased to identify the continuity of civility and moral community with that *imperium*. What they set themselves to achieve instead – often not recognizing fully what they were doing – was the construction of new forms of community.

These new forms of community were, of course, monastic, based upon a rule with an abbot and a common life of prayer and work. Our situation now is very similar because we too are at the point of failure of empires. I think it could be argued that the current crises in the British way of life derive wholly or in part from our inability or our unwillingness to accept the end of Empire and to discover – post-imperium – a new identity. Whatever our political allegiance may be there is wide agreement that recent prime ministers such as John Major and Margaret Thatcher have been reluctant, in spite of their criticisms of the past and its reliance upon class, to accept that new morally responsible forms of community life are required of us. Both of these leaders have looked back to previous imperiums (either under Churchill or under the cricket commentator Brian Johnston) but appear to have no coherent moral or communal vision for the future. Unfortunately 'classless' has increasingly come to mean 'empty'.

By saying that I simply want to show that we are at a turning point in Western civilization. This turning point is not exclusive to these islands. It applies in Russia, which is finding it difficult to accept the end of the communist empire. It applies in continental Europe where past empires are faded dreams. It applies also in America where retrenchment from empire is the commanding force. In this climate what new forms of communal life can we see?

In fact we see, once we begin to look, a remarkable resurgence. The revived community of St Benoit-sur-Loire is but one example. We probably all know of the community of Taizé, the originally Protestant but now ecumenical community in Burgundy. We know also of Christian communes of various kinds which have sprung up and died down. But do we know of the Community of Celebration in South London – an Anglican community with individuals and married couples forging a new way forward which links prayer and pentecostal praise with a rule of life and social commitment? We might know of Iona and Corrymeela, communities which look for reconciliation and peace by drawing on our Celtic roots, but do we also know of the community called 'La Pain de Vie' and many similar burgeoning new communities in France, many of them based on a rule with full acceptance of celibacy, poverty and obedience, dedicated to contemplative prayer and the service of the poor? These *nouvelles communautés* have a number of particular characteristics. They are dedicated to contemplative prayer and silence. They can include married couples and families, they can be more monastic. Devoted to the poor, with beautiful, simple worship, they are often engaged in evangelism. They sometimes attempt to bring together Jewish and Christian traditions by celebrating the Sabbath on Friday evening, and cherish a rich understanding of the law of God as a blessing, revealed in the Torah.

These are new forms of community within which the moral life is sustained at a time of breakdown. But it is not so much the external forms of these *nouvelles communautés* with which I am concerned. They are very diverse and descriptions of them are readily available. They also make themselves open and welcoming to visitors. My task is to to probe deeper into their inner significance.

Can their inner meaning be translated into something of significance for ordinary Christians today? Can the person in the parish pew who is not inclined to monasticism of a celibate kind find any inspiration for his or her faltering steps from monasticism old or new? Isn't this revival of community life in the Church just another form of withdrawal from the world? Even David Gillett, the Principal of Trinity College Bristol, in his recent book on evangelical spirituality, makes some rather side-swiping remarks about monasticism. He says,

> Whereas monasticism stands for some traditions as the epitome of the radical call of Christ to forsake all and follow him, for the evangelical this radical call cannot be left to the holy and encloistered minority.[2]

Does this 'holy and encloistered minority' have anything to say to the ordinary Christian in the pew?

Perhaps we should begin by looking at the Rule of Benedict, the source document of so much community life in the Church. And here the first thing to be remembered is that St Benedict does not stand at the beginning of the monastic life. Although celebrated as the Father of European Monasticism, he stood at a point somewhere along the development of that life, at the point when it was being regulated – hence the elaboration of a rule (Latin – *regula*). Benedict's rule comes at a point when it was felt that the incipient chaos of early monasticism needed to follow proper procedures.

Cassian, for example, upon whom Benedict relies, interprets the traditional monastic virtue of 'discernment' as being achieved by following the advice of the brethren and the rules of the elders; it is not an individual matter. Monks have to live by following the consensus, and the place of the abbot is to tell us what the consensus is and to enforce it. He says,

> True discernment is obtained only when one is truly humble. The first evidence of this humility is when everything done or thought of is submitted to the scrutiny of our elders. This is to ensure that one trusts one's judgement in nothing, that one yields to their authority in everything, that the norms for good and bad must be established in accordance with what they have handed down.[3]

This weight of tradition was first codified by the unknown 'Master' in a set of monastic rules known as

'The Rule of the Master' and then by St Benedict. Benedict certainly modifies the strict austerity of the Master's rule, but does not abandon the general thrust, which is to ensure conformity of practice. For example, The Rule of the Master tells everybody what they are supposed to be doing at any time of the day or night in any circumstances. Monks are divided into groups of ten, each with two 'provosts' – two, so that if they split into smaller groups they still have a supervisor. Nobody can go off on their own without being watched. For example, there is a short chapter telling monks to be kind to those who are sick, but a very much longer one telling them how to make sure that somebody who says he is sick really is sick! The monk who claims to be sick must be given very little food so that unless he is actually ill, hunger might drive him out of bed to look for food in the kitchen!

It has been pointed out by scholars that the Master hardly ever speaks of people wanting to live in the monastery out of love for God, and even in the one place where he does, he immediately qualifies this and talks of 'discipline and the norms of holy living'.

Benedict modifies all this austerity but he does not completely abandon it. This is not always stated by those who have realized something of the importance that monasticism has for our modern generation. There is a tendency to go overboard about St Benedict and to see him as the humane regulator who adapts all this austerity and softens it with a proper understanding of the weakness of human nature. This, of course, is seen as an attractive feature. But I think it could be very misleading to emphasize this too strongly and could lead us to miss the real point of what monastic living is all about.

This tendency can be seen in the work of Esther de Waal, an undoubted enthusiast for St Benedict. It should be said that Esther de Waal is the one who almost single-handedly, in the Anglican communion at least, has brought the Benedictine way into focus for our generation and made it accessible for Christians today; but she makes too much, in my view, of the discontinuity between the Rule of the Master and that of St Benedict. She says,

> The Rule of the Master had given enormous power to the abbot. St Benedict changes this almost exclusively vertical pattern of authority by emphasising the relationships of the monks with each other ... Textually his Rule may be almost the same in many of its phrases as that of the Master; but in its mood and outlook it is a world apart.[4]

This does really need a little modifying. If we look at the two rules we can see that Benedict does make changes – for example, he allows the monks to elect their abbot, but only with special precautions to prevent them electing somebody who will consent to their faults. He reduces the supervisory procedures for the brethren, but still requires the abbot to search the monks' beds frequently to ensure they are not keeping any private property! The point which Esther de Waal has perhaps underplayed is that in spite of the differences of emphasis the theology which lies behind these monastic rules, whether that of the Master or that of St Benedict, is really that of St Augustine.

That means that the rules contain the assumption that human minds and human wills are far too unstable and erratic, particularly it might be said, at a time of social breakdown, to form the basis for Christian discipleship on their own. St Augustine taught that human nature is inherently weak and so needs the objective support of the Church and the community and the grace of God within that community. A free and willing acceptance of community life is the only gateway to holiness.

In this rather severe way of looking at things, true freedom grows when we accept constraint, and so monastic obedience is the way of leading us to heaven by providing the circumstances within which grace can act upon us. You could say that the monastic way is understood by the Master and by Benedict as a sort of cooking pot. Community life is a deliberately enclosed pot so that gradually, by bringing the raw and recalcitrant ingredients of human nature close to the heat of God's love, the true flavour of what they contain may emerge.

This, incidentally, is the import of St Benedict's famous phrase in the Prologue to his Rule, where he says we must 'learn to run with hearts enlarged'. This has often been used by Christian teachers and retreat leaders to encourage people to live in a spirit of openness to each other and to God, and it certainly has that ring to it; but the full quotation shows that it comes from a very different context, one which is actually suspicious of our capacity to reach the goal of holiness without constraint. The phrase comes at the point where Benedict tells his monks that they must accept the discipline of the Rule,

> But if, for the correction of faults or the preservation of
> charity, some degree of restraint is laid down, then do
> not be overcome with terror . . . on the contrary,
> through the continual practice of monastic observance
> . . . our hearts are opened wide . . .[5]

In other words, the Rule of St Benedict is based on the
same principle as an arranged marriage – that if the
couple do not love each other at first then by living
together faithfully and observing all that needs to be
observed and supporting each other they will come to
do so in the end! Continually fulfilling the needs of the
rule makes you love the rule. Or, as one commentator
says, it relies upon the principle that behaving like
Christians, we actually become new creatures in Christ.

But before we become too shocked and discard St
Benedict as totally outmoded it might be worth pausing
at this point to see if such a view has any benefits. For if
this is the essence of monasticism – the acceptance of a
rule by which we are brought through to see the face
of God – then there is a relevance here for all of us who
are not subject to monastic rules but who need to place
ourselves within the discipline of the common life of the
church. For the common life of any local church can be
seen as that which replaces the acceptance of a formal
rule. Just as the monk accepts the rule and the discipline,
so the ordinary Christian accepts the limitations of the
local church community, its pettiness, but also its
opportunities. Each church community is a sort of
cooking pot. For the everyday Christian, Benedict's Rule
is not to be found so much in monastic chapters as in the
discipline of the Parish Meeting, the Church Council and
the limitations of worship in any of our churches, where

we have to learn to live with each other through thick and thin. We do not need to live in a convent or a monastery to find what Benedict calls 'a school of the Lord's service'. There is one not very far away from each one of us where, if we would accept the discipline of regular worship, of love in community and the rule of accepting others then eventually we will be able to run with hearts enlarged and find 'a sweetness of love that is beyond words'.

By looking at things in this way the normal parish then becomes the primary place of 'monastic' vocation for the Christian today, and if the meaning of the monastic way is that its participants accept the discipline of living with the people God has given us in the place where he has put us then 'the monastery' is where we already are. This, incidentally, is the reason why the French bishops are so very suspicious of the many *nouvelles communautés* which are springing up. They would say 'Look, you've already got a school of the Lord's service in parish life but these new communities are drawing people away from it.' And they would have a point.

What I am saying is that the real heirs of St Benedict and his Rule are not so much the new 'Christian communities' which are to be found in different parts of Europe but the parish communities which have always been present and which are so frequently scorned as slow and old fashioned. This is given additional force by the fact that St Benedict did not enjoin upon his monks a vow of poverty but did ask them to vow stability – that they would stay with the community in one place. Parish life, particularly Anglican parish life, with its resident priest and its attachment to 'place' is therefore in direct line with Benedict – it is the popular equivalent of a rule originally intended for a few. This is what Esther de Waal says,

> . . . we might all too easily forget the continuing link of the church of England with the Benedictine life. For the Benedictine presence, so strong in England in the Middle Ages, left its mark on the church at the time of the Reformation . . . It is hardly too much to claim that the Benedictine spirit is at the root of the Anglican way of prayer. And, if the Benedictine way stands above all else for balance and moderation, so also does the Anglican via media.

But to say that the contemporary equivalent of the monastery, for everyday Christians, is the parish, particularly the Anglican parish with its emphasis upon the importance of place, while very true and very necessary, is only part of the way in which we might reinterpret the monastic search in our own day. I hinted at a further truth when I said earlier that Benedict's Rule was only one of a series of rules – albeit the most humane – which came into existence when Western monasticism became codified and preoccupied with the need for 'proper procedures' in order to regulate the incipient chaos of a previous era. What was there, then, before that and does that have anything to say to our modern age?

What there was was a more diffused but nevertheless strong tradition of monastic life in what scholars call the eremitic rather than the coenobitic tradition. In the eremitic (from which we get our word 'hermit') life, the emphasis was upon the individual monk who had taken up the monastic way on his own or with a group of others, all of whom were striving for the divine life, but where the links between them were informal rather than formal. For example, individual monks may have resorted to a spiritual father and such spiritual fathers may have formed communal groups, but their way of life – which we know about largely from a number of stories and anecdotes known as the *Verba Seniorum*[6] – was not regulated. The coenobitic life, on the other hand, meant living and eating in community. So historically the great shift in monastic tradition was not so much between the Rule of the Master and the so-called 'humane' Rule of St Benedict, but between the individualism and apparent eccentricity of the Desert Fathers and the rules of Western monasticism.

The Desert Fathers were those Christians who flocked – and apparently it was 'flocked', for there were many – to live in the Egyptian deserts in the fourth century. There are a number of theories as to why they did this. Some suggest that the movement derives from a desire for martyrdom of the spirit when, after Christianity had become the official religion of the Empire during the reign of Constantine, physical martyrdom became an impossibility. It is suggested that in the early days of the faith martyrdom was the way to sanctity, but now that was impossible Christians sought sanctity by living impossibly ascetic or 'martyred' lives in the desert. While there may be some truth in this, it is not an interpretation upheld by most scholars of the Desert Fathers. Simon Tugwell, the Roman Catholic scholar says, 'Text after text declares that endurance and deprivation were not the major aims ... striking self-denial was pointless if it gave offence ...' This is borne out by the story about the visitor to one of the Desert Fathers who says, 'Forgive me, Father, for distracting you from your rule.' The Hermit replies, 'My rule is to put your mind at rest and to send you away in peace.'[7]

According to Simon Tugwell, the aim of the Desert Fathers was integration of the self, a rediscovery of who they really were.

> The point is this – before you can truly pray, let alone achieve any of the more refined feats of spirituality or service, you have first of all got to make sure that you are really there. And the discipline of staying in your cell (that was one of the favourite sayings of the Desert Fathers, 'Stay in your cell and your cell will teach you everything') is intended to bring you face to face with yourself and with your real needs and capacities ... Without this foundation of self-knowledge and realism, any attempt to help other people will founder ...

Thomas Merton, the American mystic, says the same and puts the Fathers in their social context. He says that it is significant that they fled to the desert at the time of the creation of the 'Christian State' under Constantine.

> What the Fathers sought most of all was their own true self, in Christ. And in order to do this, they had to reject completely the false formal self, fabricated under social compulsion in 'the world'. As Constantine christianised the Roman Empire, so the numbers of Desert Fathers grew.[8]

So however eccentric, here we have a form of monastic ideal which is prior to that of Benedict and in some people's view more essential. It is the view that the monk is the one who, above all else, seeks to come face to face with himself; who says that the quest for God will, if it is truly a quest for God, eventually bring integrity to the person. Now, I do not want to say that this cannot be done within the corporate and regulated Benedictine tradition. Obviously it can be, but the point which Merton continually made was that the monk is only distinguished from other people by virtue of the fact that he gives himself exclusively and continuously to the search for God by forsaking the normal patterns of employment and regular behaviour in the world. Others seek for God in the same way but this time within their responsibilities in this world. And so the monk is not set above others, he is simply living out his vocation.

And this is the point which the Desert Fathers would have made. Indeed the monastic life may give its follower particular problems, but the monk or nun is one who treads this path to God because he or she is called, for various reasons which may not always be easily discerned, to follow that way. In this sense the rules and structures of the monastic life are no more than aids to the discovery of the true self and may have to be adapted or changed in each generation. Regulation in itself, therefore, is not of the essence. The point is that discovery of the true self is something to which we are all called and the monk is the sign of our common vocation.

So this brings us to the central question. In the renewal of monasticism today, whether this is in renewed monastic communities like St Benoit-sur-Loire or in one of the more charismatic *nouvelles communautés*, where is spiritual guidance to be found? Despite the rise of the rule under Benedict and its subsequent triumph in Western monasticism, this question has not really been finally resolved. Is it to be found in the rule and in obedience to the rule or is there a deeper, more existential question at stake? Thomas Merton would, undoubtedly, have said, 'Yes, of course there is,' and his constant return to this question showed how much he struggled with it over the years. For him the rule was but a means of entry into the silence of God and slowly he came to see that to stand before the silence of God was the one thing necessary and that one could do this even without a rule. Merton discovered this in his own spiritual pilgrimage and sought to move his community towards a greater acceptance of the place of the individual hermit monk and eventually became one himself; but on the way came up against the whole question of control-regulation – by his abbot and his superiors. In this way he repeated within his monastery during his lifetime the historical struggle between the eremitic and coenobitic life which had taken place about the time of St Benedict.

What is important for the everyday Christian is that Merton pioneered, through his reading of the Desert Fathers and through his own spiritual struggle, a view of 'monasticism' that is translatable into the ordinary life of the individual Christian caught in the wilderness of present-day civilization, because it is one which is deeply interior. Very strikingly he anticipated the quotation from Alasdair MacIntyre with which we began this chapter when he said,

> We need another movement such as that which drew these men into the deserts of Egypt . . . we must liberate ourselves, in our own way, from involvement in a world which is plunging to disaster. We cannot do exactly as they did, but we must be as thorough and as ruthless in our determination to break all spiritual chains, to cast off the domination of alien compulsions, to find our true selves, to discover our spiritual liberty and build on earth the Kingdom of God.

Merton knew that he was called to do that by being a monk. But he also knew that this interior quest was possible and even essential in the world.

But this interior quest was not just a question of searching for God. It also involved putting a question mark over 'the world'. Merton went through a great deal of careful thinking about what he meant by 'the world'. He kept asking what we really mean by 'this world', whether we have to reject it, and what we mean by rejection. At the end of his life he came to say that the monk's relationship to this world was not so much one of rejection as that of social critic.

In his last address, given just before he died, Merton described the monk as a profound social critic who raised questions about society which society needs to hear but which society cannot generate for itself. He told of his encounter with some Marxist students, whom he thought had parallels with monasticism, and said, 'The monk is essentially someone who takes up a critical attitude towards the world and its structures.'

I remember this point being strongly made in a conversation I once had with one of the monks of Bec in France when I went there on a pilgrimage with some students. We asked him what he thought was the role of the monk. He considered for a long time and then he said 'asking questions'. The role of the monk as social critic is, however, strictly allied to the role of the monk as seeker after God alone. The monk cannot be a social critic, or remain such unless he is skewed to the world by means of his unrelenting search for God.

So the essence of monastic life and its contribution to us as ordinary Christians is to do with the search for integration, for personal and moral identity in a disintegrating world. This is done by means of an unrelenting search for God alone, sometimes within community and sometimes not. It results in the asking of questions about the nature of the society in which we live. We desperately need this today. And so the question with which we began – 'Do we need a new St Benedict?' – is a necessary one, but to answer it purely in Benedictine or in communitarian form is not sufficient. The answer lies further back than Benedict in the questions the Desert Fathers asked.

The contemporary emphasis on the importance of community life risks being somewhat overplayed. New communities can be just as oppressive as old ones. We need the monk, I believe, not so much to provide new communities as to ask radical questions about the sort of society we live in, and the monk is able to do that because he seeks without ceasing to stand before the face of God. It may well be that the only place within which such a search can be made and within which such radical questions can be safely asked is a monastic or quasi-monastic community such as the parish; but it is essential to remember that the purpose of these communities is not simply to exist but to provide the context within which such a search and such radical questioning can take place. The monk and the monastic ideal are only there to remind us as individuals of what we should be doing anyway and can do if we would . . . which is to search for God and his righteousness in the world.

FOR ACTION AND REFLECTION:

• Read the Rule of St Benedict and visit a Benedictine monastery. Ask the monks what they think they are doing. Can an ordinary lay Christian live the same vision outside of the monastery?

• Try to read about or visit a modern Christian community. Ask them what they think they are doing and see if this can apply to Christians living in the world.

• Ask yourself what you think the essence of the monastic life really is. Could it apply to you?

• Does Jesus say things in the gospels which provide a basis for the monastic life?

TWO

Biblical Holiness

I WANT TO begin by quoting from a newspaper article. It appeared in the *Independent* in the series by Danny Danziger called 'The Best of Times – The Worst of Times'. These are little articles where somebody tells you about one of their best or worst experiences. This time the contribution was from a woman journalist who at one point in her life felt that she had totally lost her faith in God. She was, or rather had been, a Catholic, had been to a convent school, but now all that meant nothing to her and she was in a dark and depressed frame of mind. It was in this depressed state that she went to be an au pair in Paris and looked after three difficult children whose mother kept retiring to bed with a sick headache. One afternoon off, she decided to go to Chartres and visit the cathedral. She writes:

> It made an incredible impression on me. I hadn't seen a lot of beautiful buildings or religious art, because convents are suspicious of too much sensuality in any shape or form, but I thought it was the most stunning thing I had ever seen. You come from the brilliance of the sun into this dark cathedral, which at the same time is glowing with a sort of light. There must have been hundreds of tourists, as it was the middle of summer, but I remember seeming to stand there alone in this

incredible half-darkness. And here was this beautiful
place, which had been made by people who believed
what I had lost. Everywhere it was telling the stories of
faith, in the carvings and in the glass. It was a sort of
living book about the faith . . .[1]

I have quoted this young woman's account at length
because it seems to me to mirror something of our
spiritual condition in the modern age. We live in a
world of depression and solitude, like this person.
Our religion has passed away. But there is still within
us a longing for the divine or the transcendent and in
order to fulfil that, this young representative of our
condition visits a cathedral. Those who theologize
about evangelism should meditate upon this young
woman as a representative of our age and what it was
that struck her. There in Chartres, she sees the cathedral building as a 'living book about the faith'.

That should not be difficult at Chartres. There you
enter, or should enter, the cathedral through the great
west door, the Royal Door, a door which although
wide at first narrows like a funnel and draws you into
the building. As you are drawn in, you are welcomed
on either side by those strange elongated figures
carved by the Master Carver of Chartres, Kings of
Israel, welcoming you into the history of the people
of God. And as you go down the aisle, the stories of
the people of God are told in stone and glass on either
side until you reach the crossing, the centre of the
heavenly Jerusalem which the medieval gothic cathedral was built to symbolize – a re-presentation of
heaven on earth.

A particular window at Chartres which has always

caught my imagination is the Good Samaritan window. The story in this window begins not with the man going from Jerusalem to Jericho but with the creation. It shows God blowing life into Adam's nostrils. Then it shows the fall, echoing how the traveller from Jerusalem to Jericho 'fell' among thieves; but then Christ, the Good Samaritan, comes and picks him up and pours the oil and wine of salvation into his wounds and brings him home. The window tells the story of our salvation just as the cathedral tells the same story.

The young secularized woman who writes the article could feel those stories as she stood there. But it is less easy, far less easy, to imagine her saying the same about the Bible itself, the book in which these stories are to be found. She – and we ourselves – can see Chartres or even other cathedrals, as a story book about the faith, but find it far less easy to see the Scriptures themselves in the same way. For a number of reasons we have lost that capacity. Indeed the Scriptures are no longer seen as a 'story book about the faith'. By and large, they are not part of the world in which we live. For us, the Scriptures are either lost completely, or deeply problematic. They may even be considered to be absolutely true, but whatever they are they are not 'a story book about the faith'.

I am fond of telling two stories to illustrate just how far away from seeing the Bible as a 'story book about the faith' we have come. They both happened in one of my parishes within a short space of time. The first concerns a woman who, after I had preached a sermon about the need for us to return to feed on the great images of Scripture, attacked me verbally, asking, 'What is all this about a return to the Bible? Surely that is a retrograde step? Surely we have moved away from the Bible and all the barbarity that it represents, particularly in this church. Surely we are now liberated from all that?' The second incident happened in the same church. Within the space of a few weeks, I was similarly attacked after preaching another sermon, but this time because I had not proclaimed the absolute truth of Scripture clearly enough. Two students fiercely asked me to provide more of what the angry lady did not want.

Those people, of course, were Christians. But even non-Christians are compelled to attempt to unravel the conundrum. One of them is Robin Lane Fox, an atheist historian who has written a book called *The Unauthorised Version*. He says that the Scriptures are the creation of Christians and Jews and have nothing divine or revelatory about them.

> The scriptures are not unerring. They are not 'The Word of God'; what we now read is sometimes only one textual version among earlier alternatives; its story may be demonstrably false; it may ascribe sayings to people which they never said. Throughout, my unauthorised version has tried to reach for what the authors meant, insisting that it can undercut what the churches, literary critics or modernising readers now claim what the scriptures mean. To christians that present meaning may be ascribed to the Holy Spirit, promised as a help in seeing what the scriptures are saying. Others may wonder if the Spirit is indeed so holy when interpretations have often been so false.[2]

And we must admit that Robin Lane Fox is certainly not alone. I have often talked with people who feel that the Scriptures are irrelevant or exercise a malignant influence upon the human spirit.

I have dwelt for some time upon our sense of loss of the Scriptures, different kinds of loss, but loss nonetheless. There is the poignant, sad loss experienced by that young woman in Chartres; the deliberate loss by the angry woman parishioner; the grasping attempt at desperate recovery by two evangelical students; and the proud academic and disdainful rejection by a secular historian who is devoted to his view of truth. All these people are part of our age. There is a real sense in which the Scriptures are 'lost' to our generation. However, I have come to believe that this loss is not inevitable, that there can be a recovery, but only if we search carefully for who we are and ask how that person, once discovered, reads the text. This is because the root of the problem lies in ourselves and how we read the Scriptures as much, if not more, than it lies within the Scriptures themselves.

The first step towards the recovery of a biblical spirituality in our day is the recovery of a different sense of time. What we need is a discontinuous sense of time. Let me explain. Those of you who read novels will either feel irritated or enriched by flashback techniques. Quite often you never seem to know whether you are here or there. An interesting exponent of this technique is the exiled Czech writer, Josef Skvorecky. Skvorecky was a colleague of Vaclav Havel, now President of the Czech Republic, and before the Velvet Revolution went into exile in Canada. Flashback occurs a great deal in his novel *The Engineer of Human Souls*. He employs the technique to compare and contrast not just the past with the present but Canada with Czechoslovakia, capitalism with communism. In a recent newspaper interview, Skvorecky said that he thought time should be seen 'hologrammatically'. An example of a hologram appears on our cheque cards, where the different symbols of the bank apparently lie behind each other, in layers, but in the same place. Hologrammatic time, therefore, is time understood in the same way, where the past is present within current events. What happened is, in a real sense, still happening, and the past cannot be divorced from the present. Skvorecky is not the only novelist or poet to expound such a viewpoint. James Joyce is another.

While we have grown used to such techniques in novels and films we are less used to finding them in religion, but a number of contemporary writers would understand spiritual experience in a similar way. One of them suggests that from a spiritual point of view we should understand that each moment incorporates the past and the future, especially if we are open to the mystery of God.[3] Each moment then contains an enormous amount from the past and is open to the future and to God. As well as novelists – Proust is, of course, the outstanding example – psychotherapists know of the way in which each action contains so much from the past; but it is only recently that such a way of understanding things has found its way into the religious domain.

So it should not be surprising to find similar ideas amongst those whose task it is to interpret the Scriptures. A particularly interesting exponent of what we might venture to call 'hologrammatic' scriptural interpretation is Timothy Radcliffe, the Master of the Dominican Order.[4] His thesis is that since the rise of the Enlightenment we have lived without hologrammatic time. What I have called hologrammatic time he calls 'true' time and contrasts that with the debased 'linear' time which was introduced at the Enlightenment by scientists such as Newton. A 'true' sense of time is one in which past and present interpenetrate one another. Instead we have lived with what he calls a 'homogeneous and empty time'. This time is the time of physics and escapement clocks and Newton. Newton said, 'Absolute, true and mathematical time, of itself and of its own nature, flows equably without relation to anything external.'

Radcliffe's view is that the biblical narratives are not written according to this view of time but according to 'true' time – a quite different pattern. He gives as an example the account in St John's Gospel of the death of Jesus.

Jesus' side is opened and out flows water and blood, just as Adam's side was opened when Eve was created. . . . And it was common in patristic exegesis to see here a reference to the New Adam bringing forth the New Eve, the church with her sacraments of baptism and eucharist. This event is not just the death of a man in the third decade of the first century. It is also the time of Creation, in which God's making of humanity comes to some sort of completion, just as is that eighth day after the Resurrection when Jesus will breathe the Holy Spirit on the disciples as God breathed his Spirit on the first Adam so that he became a living being. But yet another time is evoked. John has advanced the time of Jesus' death, as given by the synoptic tradition, by twenty-four hours so that now he dies at the same time as the Paschal lambs are slaughtered in the Temple; the Temple liturgy also laid down that their limbs are not to be broken. This is the time of the new Exodus from sin and death. So three times are evoked – of Creation, of the Exodus, of the slaughter of Paschal lambs, to describe the death of this man on the hill.

The Johannine narratives are, of course, particular examples of this 'true' or 'hologrammatic' time, where the past exists within the present. Radcliffe's important point is that the biblical narratives are not written with the same sense of the 'passing of time' that we have possessed since the Newtonian revolution. They are written to a different pattern and we will always fail to understand them unless we see them and read them in that light.

One of the major reasons why we have 'lost' the Scriptures is our inability to read them from this point of view. We read them looking for the wrong things. We ask, for example, 'Did it happen in this way?' 'Is this a true history?' 'If there was a reporter there at the time, would he have written this?' And when we ask those questions, we shall always be disappointed, for the answer to all of them is almost always 'no' in the plain sense in which the question is asked.

Linked to this Newtonian view of time is a related question. Once you believe that time is always linear and passes, then you become no more than the observer of this process. A quest for historical 'truth' in Scripture not only presupposes a certain view of time which is not shared by the Scriptures, it also presupposes that the scriptural writers are disengaged observers and that these observers wrote down what they saw happening as if they had been passing by at the time. But once again this is not how the gospels came to be written. They were written by people whose immediate motive for writing was their experience of the resurrection of Jesus and their sense that they participated in this resurrection. They are written from the resurrection. For them the resurrection is not over and done with, it continues, hologrammatically as it were, within their own ecclesial experience. Another Dominican makes this point when he says,

> The New Testament is the apostolic witness set down in writing ... that witness is not merely a witness to the fact of the resurrection, though it certainly is that ... even more than that it is witness from the resurrection. That is to say it was a happening which profoundly changed them.[5]

But if that is how the gospels were written, from within the resurrection, then that is how they must be read. We may try to read them as history but we cannot do that without falsifying what is being said. Moreover, it is not just the writers who stood within a certain experience, but we too, the readers. For we too have a hologrammatic element within us and we always bring to the reading of Scripture a person, ourselves, who already stands within a particular way of life. My point is that we will only be able to read the texts fully and properly, only be able to recover them, when we accept that that is the case and own it. In other words, we have to accept that the 'disengaged reader', as well as the 'disengaged writer' – both people standing back from the facts and looking down upon them from above – do not exist. We are all participants of different kinds and at different levels.

It is also worth remembering that there is increasing evidence that the concept of the 'disengaged observer' – whether the observer is the one who writes or the one who reads – is also, strangely enough, at the root of fundamentalist readings of Scripture. For the fundamentalist always or usually draws disengaged conclusions from the text. He knows what happened because the text, divinely given, says what it says. Yes, it did happen as it says, what I am seeing in the text is exactly what the writer saw. Fundamentalism thus reveals itself to be allied to an understanding of the evangelists as disengaged observers and the reader as being a disengaged reader. This betrays the fact that it is a purely modern phenomenon, despite claims to be the 'true' way of reading, and so just as shot through with modern preconceptions about how we come to know things as the liberalism which it purports to criticize.

If we are not careful we might also forget that not only is the disengaged observer difficult to find, but even when we find one he or she is not really free. Nobody is entirely free from the influence of the age in which they live and the controlling philosophies of the day. A reader might think that by espousing literalist or fundamentalist readings of the Scriptures they are setting themselves free from the risks of 'personal interpretation' – the sin of liberalism. But in reality they are only putting themselves straight into the hands of whatever the dominant economic and political philosophy might be (whether to the right or to the left, it makes no odds), without any chance of defending themselves from its worst consequences through the exercise of their own personal judgement. Awareness of and ownership of my own choices is the only final guarantee of my freedom from alienation by the dominant political or economic power of the time. Personal freedom is the final bastion against fascism as well as communism. The one who thinks they can (or, indeed, need) only observe is also the one who, ultimately, has forfeited his will and has become absorbed into the ruling force of the day. Such a person will, in the end, do what the ruling force does. In the West at present this will mean that the text will be predominantly presented as something to enhance personal well-being. The text will be reduced to the consumerism of our day, and become no more than another artefact which we consumer hungry people need. Its inner message will be overridden. Once again we see how fundamentalism is nothing more than a capitulation to the modernism it purports to deny.

Another group of people who have attempted to recover our sense of belonging to the text of Scripture are those dubbed 'feminist' critics. Many of the more recent feminist readings of the Scripture begin by a rejection of a way of reading that relies upon the 'disengaged observer' of so-called 'higher', 'scientific' or 'historical' criticism. What feminist scholarship demonstrates is the demise of a way of reading Scripture which, while it purported to be objective and scientific, was in fact no more than an extension of Western male dominated consumerism. One of the best of these scholars – Sandra Schneiders – makes the point that the adoption of the scientific method as the only possible method of interpreting Scripture actually produces a predetermined set of results.

> When method controls thought and investigation the latter may lead to accurate data but it does not lead to truth. Method, understood as a pre-established set of procedures for investigating some phenomenon, in fact not only attains its object but creates its object ... it determines a priori what kind of data can be obtained and will be considered relevant.[6]

In other words if the concept of the disengaged observer is the ruling one, then only disengaged facts will emerge.

And so the primary reason why we have lost the Scriptures is that we have given ourselves over to an alien mind-set involving linear time and a disengaged observer of that time. We have been unwilling to rest happy with reading the text in what I have called a hologrammatic way, listening to the resonances, seeing the connections and the metaphors and allowing ourselves to be part of them. So a distance has been created which has kept us from being part of what is read. We have ended up in the position of the young lady in Chartres, out of the story, always disengaged from the story, always saying 'It's over there, it belongs to somebody else, it belongs to another time.'

I think we can recover this 'true' sense of time only if we take a long and serious look at how human beings find their identity. Human beings derive their identity, I would suggest, from the story that bears them and the stories that they tell. Christians, for example, are those who carry within them and proclaim by word and deed the story of Jesus, particularly the story of his death and his resurrection. They live out this story and affirm its truth not just historically but also by performing it in their own lives. Each Sunday the Christian community gathers to hear the stories of Jesus again, to remember what he did and what he said. They also gather to remember him in the breaking of bread and to be re-membered, or put together again, by re-enacting that story. The Hebrew for re-member carries a much stronger weight than modern English and virtually means to re-present or to re-happen. At Easter the Christian community re-members the last days of Jesus' life by re-telling the Passion Story day by day and re-enacting what happened. Thus they identify the story that carries them, which they belong to, and which shapes their existence. When at the Easter vigil the stories of redemption are told and the Paschal Candle is lit, the action re-presents Christ and re-stores him to his place in the community and re-members the community as the crucified and risen community. It is not a question of remembering that such and such happened two thousand years ago as if all we had to do was to recall the past to mind. No, it is a question of identifying again with the action and entering into the text, of becoming the text of the story once again now. Then the drama of death and resurrection and the saving, victorious action of God in Christ will be played out not just by us but in us.

Now I think that it is a pity that Christian communi-

ties in the West only re-present the Christian stories at
Easter and perhaps in nativity plays at Christmas. The
Ethiopian Orthodox Church celebrates the stories of
its identity a great deal more vigorously. At Epiphany,
the archbishops are showered with water as a sign of
their re-baptism, because this is the feast of the Baptism of Christ. At Easter, they do not just light a
Paschal Candle, they send people looking for the body
of Jesus all over the cathedral at Aksum. People go
hunting for the body and then come back saying, 'No,
he is not here, he is risen.' This is a re-enactment of
the story. Our capacity to see ourselves as the community which bears and re-members the story of Jesus
has been diminished, if not lost, by an understanding
of Scripture as fact, or maybe error, read by the
disengaged reader possessed of a linear sense of time.
All those things have taken away our capacity to be
part of the story.

In the chapter on the search for monastic holiness I
mentioned the Roman Catholic scholar, Alasdair Mac-
Intyre and his important book *After Virtue*. He says
somewhere else in that book,

> Man is essentially a story-telling animal . . . I can only
> answer the question 'What am I to do?' if I can answer
> the prior question 'Of what story or stories do I find
> myself a part?' . . . Deprive children of stories and you
> leave them unscripted, anxious stutterers in their actions
> as in their words. Hence there is no way to give us an
> understanding of any society, including our own, except
> through the stock of stories which constitute its initial
> dramatic resources. Mythology, in its original sense, is
> at the heart of things.

Part of the reason why we cannot see the Scriptures as 'Our Story' is because we read them wrongly. We do not read them as story but as words which must be analysed for their meaning. Again, part of the reason for this is the way we read. We read fast, in order to obtain information. Speed reading is a Western invention designed to enable us to pick up what is said to be essential. It is the very opposite of that great monastic practice, *lectio divina*, whereby the words are read slowly, chewed over, with all of the depths of meaning savoured, and the very hologrammatic quality of the text, with its different layers, allowed to resonate within the soul. An American Jesuit scholar, William Shannon, has written about the importance of Scripture reading as part of our quest for a true spirituality. He speaks of the importance of lectio divina in a study of the medieval treatise *The Ladder of Monks*. The ladder is, of course, the ladder of the soul to God. The third rung on the ladder is reading – 'a careful study of the scriptures in which a person's whole attention is engaged'. Shannon contrasts monastic reading or lectio divina with plain lectio which is what we moderns go in for. He says

> In an age wherein books are available in large numbers, it is important to understand how lectio divina differs from simple lectio. Whereas lectio aims at answering questions and satisfying the curiosity of the mind, lectio divina aims more at challenging the heart. While it would be wrong to think of lectio divina as anti-intellectual, it would be equally wrong to think that its purpose is simply to communicate knowledge or information . . . The final goal of lectio divina is to initiate and deepen

the conversion process in the one who reads. It seeks to draw the reader even more fully into union with Christ Jesus.[7]

And so it is important, when reading the Scriptures, to allow them the fullness of their life, to let them drop like rain on the dry ground of our souls. We should read them slowly and attentively, perhaps even mouthing them to ourselves. Our house groups should allow them space to speak, reading them twice or even three times. They should be read more as poetry, allowing the complexity of their imagery to permeate our beings. There should be silence after the Scriptures are read liturgically. All these are ways of allowing the Scriptures to live more in our midst and to re-speak their message.

While we may still have the Scriptures in our hands, we have, in a different sense, lost them because we have little understanding or sensibility of the depths and complexities of what they are. Their power as Word to us has been damaged. Consequently a spirituality of the Scriptures is lost and our search for holiness is under-resourced. We have to do it, we think, always in our minds. I do not think we can begin to be holy unless we re-enter the text and the imagery of the scriptural revelation. Our lives are laid waste unless we have deep within us a stock of archetypal poetic images. At the moment we hop from one set of pictures to another. We become mindless or we become full of garbage. The well of our psyche has to be fed by the archetypal patterns found within the text.

Unfortunately, this fills some people with deep

foreboding. They are happier to exist, it seems, without images, or with a plethora of meaningless images, rather than inhabit the biblical metaphors and so come to God. It filled the woman in my church of whom I spoke earlier with a great deal of foreboding because, I think, she was a refugee from certain types of fundamentalism and was afraid it was coming back to hit her. We do not want to be like that, and talk of returning to the archetypal patterns and metaphors of Scripture can therefore appear threatening. We fear that we will be dragged back into darkness and irrationality.

This is not what will happen. What will happen is that we will live more clearly and surely in the way we were intended to live, that is by myth, symbol and story – by owned and recognized myths, symbols and stories. Human beings actually live by myth, symbol and story in any case, but because of the excessive emphasis on 'truth' in our culture, we do not know by which myth, symbol or story we are living. We live on the surface of rationality and the stories or myths which actually dominate our behaviour are submerged in our psyche. I am sure that many people who have convinced themselves that rationally they are Christian and accept the rational truth of the Christian position are actually living by a number of unexamined assumptions which need to see the light of day. This was particularly true of Nazi Germany before the war. Here was an ostensibly Christian nation, listening carefully to the teaching of renowned liberal Christian scholars, with a strong and well organized ecclesial system, but unwittingly living by a number of unexamined myths and symbols. When the right conditions came for these myths to be adopted by those in power this adoption was only opposed by a small minority and caused the most enormous suffering.

We all live by and with myths. Most of the time these are completely beneficial, but because they are unacknowledged and unowned, some of the more demonic myths which do exist within us – racial hatred myths, male superiority myths, female inferiority myths, class myths, money myths, pleasure myths – do have the power to arise and take over our lives without notice. And all the time we say we believe in God. This is the point. I want us to live completely by the myths and symbols which God has given us ... and to own them. It is not so much a question that all myths are dark and irrational, but of which ones are dark and which are not and what we are doing to choose. And unless we develop a spirituality of the Scriptures, owning and living the scriptural images, we will not allow the Scriptures to permeate our deepest selves and will actually be living by other 'stories' which are potentially quite demonic.

Unfortunately it is the fundamentalists who are at fault in this. Their philosophy is linked to a refusal of myth or symbol or story, replacing them with the search for absolute truth. Such a quest obscures the beauty and poetic depth of the Scriptures. Much Christian fundamentalism, for example, undervalues the Hebrew Scriptures because it believes they are part of the old dispensation while the New Testament is about grace. Much of this is seen to be nonsense once we have divested ourselves of the view that the Scriptures must be read from the point of view of acquiring

'truth' which can then be expressed in some proposi-
tional form. This happened to me when, in a period
of my life when I was working closely with the
Jewish community, I came to see with fresh eyes how
the psalms were beautiful, and the Torah was a blessing. I also came to see, if I did not know already, how
the God of the Hebrew Scriptures was a God of
blessing, who brought the creation into being and
whose word undergirds all things. Perhaps if we read
the Scriptures more through such Jewish eyes, then
we will see that it is full of light.

For example, we might see that the two most
important themes in the Scriptures are creation and
consummation. God in his goodness has made all
things well. He has made all things and delights in all
things. We will see Psalm 104, the great creation
psalm which celebrates the wonder of all that is in
being, as a key text. And then we will begin to allow
the beauty of what we fear to penetrate deeper into
ourselves. Walter Brueggemann, the great Old Testament scholar, says that these twin central themes in
Scripture of creation and consummation directly con-
tradict the amnesia and despair of modern civilization.[8]
We live in forgetfulness and cynicism always wanting
not to know because we think nothing can be different. Reading the Scriptures wakens within us the
memory of our source in God, creation, and points us
to our finished state in God, consummation. It also
reminds us that while we journey we are sustained by
love. Reading Scripture then also becomes not just
an affirmation of God, creator and sustainer, but almost
a political act, an act of protest against the despair of
the world in which we live.

I would like to end with two stories to illustrate how we can become the text and take upon us scriptural holiness. The first story I have told elsewhere,[9] but it is very important. My wife and I were once part of a Bible study group in Africa. It was at a time when the Kenyan government was beginning to flex its muscles, and had passed a law requiring all aliens to register. We all had to go and report as aliens and sign up. And it happened that at that time in the Bible study group we were reading Isaiah 40–66 week by week, taking turns to introduce the passage. When it was my turn I looked up the commentaries and produced what I felt then was an intellectually satisfying account of the different theories of the Suffering Servant. I had a sharp disagreement with another priest in the group who led us through what he felt was the historical truth of the passages. Two Roman Catholic sisters came next. They led us through their section of the text asking us simply to think about it for ourselves and share our reactions. At first I thought this was Bible study for softies. But I soon began to realize that they had read the commentaries, they had read the text at an intellectual level. I was won over because all of us came away seeing the text in a new way. It was a text about us. It was a text about exile. All of us, expatriates in a foreign land, came away meditating upon new paths through the wilderness, full of the song of the exiles as they looked for the new Jerusalem. We had been fed. For that moment, we became the text. The sisters in their quiet way, by helping us to identify with the text, had enabled us all to transcend the differences between us, to forget what the Enlightenment had taught us and 'to enter the story'.

Then, lastly, let me tell you what happened to the young woman who visited Chartres Cathedral whose story I told at the beginning of this chapter. She returned to the cathedral some years later. She knew that in the stone floor of the cathedral there was a maze – a journey in stone said to symbolize the pilgrimage to Jerusalem. In the Middle Ages, pilgrims who could not go to Jerusalem itself followed this maze and went on the journey metaphorically. And so, one morning, very early in the half light and in the stillness, she followed this journey – taking off her shoes to walk barefoot upon the stones. And so she says she came back to faith. Not to a fully orthodox faith, but a faith nonetheless. She followed the story herself and allowed the story to become her.

FOR ACTION AND REFLECTION:

• Choose a passage from one of the Gospels, preferably from John's Gospel to start with, and see if you can discern all of the hints of other scriptural passages that it contains. Build your own 'hologram' of the passage. You might find a commentary helpful.

• If you go to a Bible study group think about how the group reads the Scriptures and suggest that they try to read more slowly, perhaps several times, before commenting. Encourage the group to use dramatic techniques, turning the text into a small play for the evening, as a substitute for talking about it.

• Read one of the books of the Bible in the same way that you read a novel. Don't ask yourself what it means 'religiously'. Let yourself enjoy the story and think about the characters and the way their life develops.

• Think which of the biblical stories is essentially your story. Ask yourself or your group why that is so.

THREE

Mystical Holiness

DURING A LENT study group in one of my parishes we were talking about the delight which we can have in the creation and the delight with which God regards his creation. We read one or two of the psalms, such as Psalm 104, and other scriptural passages which speak of this. Suddenly, one of the participants, a woman of some experience and clearly somebody of sturdy common sense and wisdom, told the group about an experience of hers some years before in which everything had been quietly lit from within by divine light. The people she encountered and even the very buildings she passed were fresh and new. She was filled with joy and peace. As she spoke I realized that she was describing a mystical experience in which she had glimpsed the divine presence. Afterwards I found that what she had described was not at all abnormal. In fact research shows that what came to her comes to very many people at some point in their lives.

Mysticism has not disappeared from the modern world. Those who may at one time have expected that a rational, critical and essentially non-mysterious version of Christianity would settle over the Western world and mercifully relieve it of all superstition, mystical awareness and similar psychological excesses have been gravely disappointed. Every day we hear of experiences such as that recounted by the lady in the Lent study group. Almost every day we see or hear reports of its presence, indeed its resurgence, even in the most sensible circles. Books on mysticism proliferate and suddenly everybody is talking about it.

This is, of course, remarkable by any account. Only twenty or thirty years ago the mainstream church consciousness was broadly ecumenical and essentially practical in temper. Co-operation, good works and service, at home and abroad, was the order of the day. There was a plain piety about, which eschewed experience and elevated action. These were the days when Dag Hammarskjold, while Secretary General of the United Nations, wrote in his diary, 'In our day the road to holiness inevitably lies through the world of action.' The emphasis on action shows that mystical experience was still regarded as something in the past or a private matter for those who felt led to such a thing. It was not thought to have any real import for the life of the churches.

Indeed, mystical experience was even thought to be risky, an indulgence in which might warp or disturb the judgement of sensible, action orientated Christians. Listen to these words from the Report of the Church of England Doctrine Commission which are as recent as 1987:

Those who believe in God ... testify to a variety of 'religious experiences' from a general sense of the holy or numinous, on the one hand, to a sensation of being directly addressed by a transcendent being, on the other. Moreover, not only is such experience open to the charge of being subjective, it also appears to be unequal if not haphazard in its distribution. Many profound believers claim to be ignorant of it; many powerful experiences fail to result in a solid faith . . . such experience is often ambiguous.[1]

The deeply sceptical tone of these remarks towards 'religious experiences' was not uncommon at that time and it is interesting to try and see why there has been such a shift of feeling over recent years. There are a number of fairly obvious contributory factors. One of these is the growth of pentecostal experience within the mainstream churches. This is accompanied by a rapid growth in the retreat movement, especially amongst evangelicals and nonconformists. It has been recognized for some time that those on the more catholic wing of the churches will try to find time for a quiet day or a retreat, but this has now spread to those churches which some years ago would have found such activity difficult. Evangelical Christians increasingly find the need for spiritual direction and talk of the importance of contemplative prayer.

There is also – and I believe this to be a major factor – a much deeper awareness of the presence of evil and tragedy in the world. The easy, practical optimism of a previous age has gone. Our confidence that rational religion was sufficient – indeed not just sufficient, but the very best sort of religion – has been severely dented by world events. We know that the problems we face are much greater and much more longstanding, and their eradication much more difficult.

Another factor influencing the disappearance of the practical religion fostered by the 1960s and 1970s is our awareness that religious and mystical experience is much more widespread in Western society than we had recognized. We may have thought that it had all but disappeared but the scientific evidence is to the contrary. The Alistair Hardy Unit on Research into Religious Experience was set up in the late 1970s to pursue views put forward by Hardy in his book entitled, significantly, *The Spiritual Nature of Man.*[2] This unit conducted a large number of interviews and collected a great deal of evidence from people in all walks of life and of all faiths and none about their personal experience of God. What is clear from the evidence collected is that most people do have religious or even deeply mystical experiences, which, when they have had a chance to reflect on and think about, they value and live by. What people do not do is relate these experiences very closely to church life. The institutional life of the churches and religious experience is often disconnected.

These findings have recently been supported by a Marc Europe survey about why people do not go to church. It is clear that people do not stay away from church, at least according to this quite comprehensive survey, because of lack of belief in God or lack of awareness of God or even lack of faith in Jesus Christ, but because of the behaviour of the institution. In any case what we now know is that religious or mystical experiences are extremely commonplace and much more formative in people's lives than the comments of the 1987 Doctrine Commission would suggest. We are also becoming much more aware that such experiences are well known to the artist or to the poet and, once again, the artist or the poet has been the guardian of these 'experiences' in a way which the Church, sadly, has not.[3] Apart from a few isolated and celebrated examples – such as that of Dean Hussey of Chichester who ensured that his cathedral became a home for artistic expression – the link between artistic and religious experience has been broadly lost. Witness to this is the recent inability of the dean of one English cathedral to accept within the cathedral for an exhibition the strikingly beautiful sculpture of a naked man. Witness also the general lack of contemporary artistic expression in our parish churches.

The point I am labouring is that moments of overwhelming religious experience are remarkably common. They have always been there. It is not that modern life removes them or makes them unnecessary, but that modern life makes them difficult to talk about. But listen to this account, originally quoted by Alistair Hardy in his book, *The Spiritual Nature of Man*, of how an aesthetic experience quickly became a deeply religious one.

A friend persuaded me to go to Ely Cathedral to hear a performance of Bach's B Minor Mass. I had heard the work, indeed I knew Bach's choral works pretty well . . . The music thrilled me, until we got to the great Sanctus. I find this experience difficult to define. It was primarily a warning – I was frightened. I was trembling from head to foot and wanted to cry. Actually I think I did. I heard no 'voice' except the music; I saw nothing; but the warning was very definite. I was not able to interpret this experience satisfactorily until I read some months later Otto's book, *The Idea of the Holy*. Here I found it: the 'numinous'. I was before the Judgement Seat. I was being weighed in the balance and found wanting.[4]

Let us just remain with these experiences for a moment longer before we try to talk about them. That particular moment in Ely Cathedral brought the person who experienced it into the realm of Judgement. Others are no less intense but perhaps a little more positive.

My first remembered experience of the numinous occurred when I was barely three. I recall walking down a little cul-de-sac lane behind our house in Shropshire. The sun was shining, and as I walked along the dusty lane, I became acutely aware of the things around me. I noticed a group of dandelions on my left at the base of the stone wall. Most of them were in full bloom, their golden heads irradiated by the sun, and suddenly I was overcome by an extraordinary feeling of wonder and joy. It was as if I was part of the flowers and stones and dusty earth. I could feel the dandelions pulsating in the sunlight and experienced a timeless unity with all life. It is quite impossible to express this in words or to recall its intensity. All I know now is that I knew something profound and eternal then.

That description mirrors very much that of the lady in the parish Lent group which I recalled at the beginning of this chapter. Their words could be interchangeable, they also have a Wordsworthian quality about them, recalling his lines:

There was a time when meadow, grove and stream,
The earth and every common sight,
To me did seem
Apparelled in celestial light,
The glory and the freshness of a dream.[5]

In 'The Prelude', his semi-autobiographical poem, Wordsworth goes further into this experience and detects within it a personal force which actually is at work in his life and in the universe. He learns to trust that force as being for good.

Dust as we are, the immortal spirit grows
Like harmony in music; there is a dark
Inscrutable workmanship that reconciles
Discordant elements, makes them cling together
In one society.

This deep sense of being at one with a power which is secretly at work to 'reconcile discordant elements, making them cling together in one society', is vividly illustrated in the diaries of one Admiral Byrd who manned an Antarctic weather station in 1934. He asked to go there alone, not because he was unhappy – he was actually a very successful and outwardly contented man; nor because he wanted to be a meteorologist – he was already a meteorologist of some distinction. He simply wanted space in his life. His life was, he said, 'a crowding confusion'. 'I wanted something more than just privacy in the geographical sense. I wanted to sink roots into some replenishing philosophy.' In his diary he records:

Took my daily walk at 4pm today in 89° of frost . . . I paused to listen to the silence . . . the day was dying, the night was being born, but with great peace. Here were imponderable processes and forces of the cosmos . . . harmonious and soundless. Harmony, that was it! That was what came out of the silence – a gentle rhythm, the strain of a perfect chord, the music of the spheres perhaps. It was enough to catch that rhythm, momentarily to be myself a part of it . . . In that instant I could feel no doubt of man's oneness with the universe . . .[6]

Unfortunately Admiral Byrd became ill through carbon monoxide poisoning from the stove which he kept in his hut, but not before he had written that he felt 'more alive' than at any time in his life. And when he returned home, he wrote:

I did take away something that I had not fully possessed before: appreciation of the sheer beauty and miracle of being alive, and a humble set of values . . . I live more simply now, and with more peace.

You may have seen a recent television programme which featured people who had been kept hostage or in solitary captivity for considerable periods of time in different parts of the world. It did not include Terry Waite or John McCarthy or Brian Keenan, but a number of other, lesser known, people. What was interesting was the effect that the experience had upon them afterwards. There was a rather hedonistic journalist who became very serious, returned to church, and became quasi-mystical, much to the puzzlement of his wife. There was another man who mended his marriage. There were all sorts of examples. And Brian Keenan, whose account of his captivity includes moments of sheer mystical awareness,[7] now lives on the West Coast of Ireland in semi-seclusion. They 'live more simply now and with more peace'. Admiral Byrd's experience is not so unusual – what is unusual is the depth of deprivation – voluntarily going to live in the Antarctic – that he felt he had to undergo before such an experience could be his. Modern civilized life denied it to him.

Others, particularly poets, have not had to go so far to experience something of the transfiguration which Byrd writes about. Two poets in the English tradition who write about this are Thomas Traherne and Edwin Muir. Traherne was a country rector in Herefordshire, at Credenhill, and wrote at the time of the Restoration. His 'Centuries' are a miracle of awareness of the divine within all things. He writes poetry, but best is his prose, especially this classic passage from his third set of Centuries where the whole creation, including the people he sees, are transfigured by the inward light and love of God.

The corn was orient and immortal wheat, which never should be reaped nor was ever sown. I thought it had stood from everlasting to everlasting. The dust and stones of the street were as precious as gold. The gates were at first the end of the world; the green trees when I saw them first through one of the gates transported and ravished me; Their sweetness and unusual beauty made my heart to leap and almost mad with ecstasy, they were such strange and wonderful things ... The men! O what venerable and reverend creatures did the aged seem! Immortal cherubim! and young men glittering and sparkling angels and maids strange seraphic pieces of life and beauty ... Boys and girls tumbling in the street and playing were moving jewels ... Eternity was manifest in the light of day and something infinite behind everything appeared which talked with my expectation and moved my desire.[8]

Some two hundred and fifty years later a quite different person, Edwin Muir, a Presbyterian from the Orkneys, writes in a similar way, in his poem 'The Transfiguration'.

> So from the ground we felt that virtue branch
> Through all our veins till we were whole, our wrists
> As fresh and pure as water from a well,
> Our hands made new to handle holy things,
> The source of all our seeing rinsed and cleansed
> Till earth and light and water entering there
> Gave back to us the clear unfallen world.
> We would have thrown our clothes away for lightness,
> But that even they, though sour and travel stained,
> Seemed, like our flesh, made of immortal substance,
> ... Was it a vision?
> Or did we see that day the unseeable
> One glory of the everlasting world
> Perpetually at work, though never seen
> Since Eden locked the gate that's everywhere
> And nowhere?[9]

This sort of experience is also known to artists – and in this tradition are the Shoreham etchings of Samuel Palmer and, especially, the work of the Wiltshire Quaker, Robin Tanner. His etching 'Harvest Festival' combines the stillness of adoration with a deep sense of the presence of God in all things. These artists want to 'make visible' what is invisible, without destroying what is visible in so doing.

This brief overview of mystical or transcendental experiences in the modern age cannot ignore those of Thomas Merton, the American Trappist. In his journal *Conjectures of a Guilty Bystander*, Merton gives an account of one of his central experiences which occurred after he had been in the monastery at Gethsemani for some eighteen years. It bears much resemblance to the accounts of Traherne and Muir. Merton was in Louisville to see about some printing for the monastery. He writes,

In Louisville at the corner of Fourth and Walnut, in the centre of the shopping district, I was suddenly overwhelmed with the realisation that I loved all those people, that they were mine and I theirs, that we could not be alien to one another even though we were total strangers. It was like waking from a dream of separateness, of spurious self-isolation in a special world, the world of renunciation and supposed holiness.[10]

William Shannon, Merton's biographer, comments that this experience, often recounted, sums up many of Merton's other mystical experiences.

This vision could be described as a kind of theophany, as he sees the spark of divinity in each of these persons. 'It was as if I suddenly saw the secret beauty of their hearts, the person that each one is in God's eyes.' He reflects that if only they could see themselves as they are, if only all of us could see each other that way all the time, war and hatred and greed would disappear from the face of the earth. In fact, if we truly saw one another as we are in God, we would almost be ready to kneel down and adore.[11]

Which reminds me of the Hasidic saying that in front of each person, preceding them down the street, are two angels. These angels are calling out 'Make way, make way, make way for the image of God.'

I have recounted these contemporary mystical experiences in order to demonstrate plainly, first of all, that such experiences are commonplace. They happen to all of us in the midst of the most ordinary circumstances. They are not restricted to those who are 'mystics'. Second, I have wanted to show that what ordinary people experience in these moments is not different from what poets, artists and professional religious people such as Thomas Merton experience. Then, third, it is clear that these experiences are deeply luminous in the lives of these people, they are formative for them and they want to go on living under their influence. In other words, although the 1987 Doctrinal Commission may have been right to say that these experiences are 'haphazard', in the sense that they cannot be predicted and so come to us suddenly, the Commission was not right when it said that these experiences are ambiguous or fail to result in a solid faith. Precisely the opposite seems to be true. So, just as in a previous chapter we saw that monasticism is alive and well in the twentieth century, and just as we tried to show that biblical living is alive and well, so also mystical awareness is alive and well in our own day. What do we make of this?

Perhaps we can look a little more closely at these experiences and try to understand them with a little help from the Christian tradition, because even if sceptics allow that they are more common and more formative than they thought, they may still believe that they are in some way misleading and that the important thing is not so much religious experience as religious truth. After all, they will say, all of us have minds and can grasp the truth – which is a typically modern assumption – but not everybody seems to have these experiences, even if they are more common than we had realized. What we need, the sceptic will say, is lives based upon what we know to be true rather than on what some people experience.

Furthermore, even if one is religious, can these experiences be such as to lead us to the truth about Jesus? Where does he come in? And are they not just 'experiences'? Do they really do any good? Do they really change the world or are they not simply pleasurable sensations which leave things in just as much a mess as they were before? Can being a mystic help to solve the Third World's problems, or even our own?

In looking at mystical experience the first thing we do have to realize, if we are to understand it properly, is that mystical awareness of God is not awareness of God as separate from his creation, as if God was a special sort of being who was 'seen' by special people by means of 'special' experiences. In other words Christian theology does not support the view that there are certain 'religious' people who possess a special 'religious receptivity' which enables them to tune in to God, while other people lack this faculty. This is actually quite a difficult point for us to come to terms with, partly because of the popular view that religious experience comes to only a few, particularly privileged people.

Let us look at some of the theology behind this in the words of Rowan Williams, Bishop of Monmouth. He writes,

> The Christian God is not an object in the universe and is not, therefore, a possible competitor for space in it. So it would not be true to say that we sometimes experience God 'neat' as it were, and sometimes at second-hand . . . All our experience is experience of the world – of things, of persons. Experience of God is to learn to see these things and these persons in a certain context – a context for which we can never find adequate description and which must never be reduced to being one item among others.[12]

In another place, Bishop Williams takes issue with the idea that mysticism is really a special sort of experience. He says,

> Mysticism should not be taken to describe a cross-cultural, supra-credal specific experience, but a jumble of attempts to perceive how consciousness is drastically reconditioned by the living out in depth of a particular religious commitment.[13]

By that I take it that he is trying to say that if you live the faith through and through you will begin to 'see' things differently or may have moments when you 'see' things differently, perhaps because you have been looking at everything, or trying to look at everything, from the point of view of God. Your inner eye has been opened and you begin to be able to see everything as it really is. But you are still the same person, and still the same person looking at the same reality.

Perhaps I can clarify this a bit further by talking about the work of a modern Catholic theologian, Baron von Hügel. Von Hügel was an aristocratic Catholic thinker who lived in London at the turn of the century and wrote very quaint letters of spiritual direction to his niece and a lot of philosophy of religion. He sought valiantly to rehabilitate the 'mystical' element in religion, but knew that its definition was fraught with difficulty. He made an interesting and important distinction between 'inclusive' and 'exclusive' mysticism.

What he called exclusive mysticism is the sort of mysticism in which the soul finds itself alone with God in a unitive experience. This is probably what most ordinary Christians would regard as the real thing, but he regarded it as mistaken. That was because it tends to suggest that human experience of this world is a distraction from the real task of knowing God. We have to 'exclude' ourselves from experience and normal reality in order to find God. Inclusive mysticism, on the other hand, is that sort of mysticism which is reflected in the extracts which have been quoted earlier in this chapter, where the world is shot through with a divine light and the person experiences a total unity with that transfigured world. In this 'inclusive' view all human experience has a hidden potential for bearing God and sees nothing as wasted and everything as a potential gateway for God. In other words inclusive mysticism is a living of life at its greatest possible depth. Inclusive mysticism would also reject the view that there is a separate mystical faculty in the human personality by which we may know God.

Von Hügel says that whereas all mysticism contains a 'turning away from all multiplicity and contingency, from the visible and successive in a single-minded quest for the one thing necessary, the pearl of great price, the glimpsed simplicity and stillness, the eloquent silence of the mystery of God', an 'exclusive' mysticism will pursue this goal to the exclusion of reality, but 'inclusive' mysticism will do it through reality. I must admit that my observation of so many people on retreat when I was the director of a retreat and conference centre, and my conversations with so many people who are engaged upon the spiritual quest, lead me to know something of the truth and relevance of von Hügel's distinction. So many of them came with the sole intention of completely forgetting about whatever it was that was troubling them, of escaping to the comfort and security of a retreat house. I am sure that the respite did them good and they returned to their daily lives better able to tackle these difficulties, but what they were not looking for was a transfiguring of their experience, rather an obliteration of it.

A similar distinction is made by the Danish thinker Kierkegaard in his description of what he calls the Knight of Faith. Kierkegaard was an unusual man who lived a reclusive existence but who, perhaps through his reclusiveness, came to understand something of the deeply interior and hidden nature of faith. In a famous essay, *Fear and Trembling,* he talks about the Knight of Faith who renounces the finite yet continues to live in it. The Knight of Faith

> . . . takes delight in everything and whenever one sees him taking part in a particular pleasure he does it with the persistence which is the mark of the earthly man. He looks and acts like a tax collector and yet the man has made and every instant is making the movements of infinity. He resigned everything infinitely, and then he grasped everything again by virtue of the absurd . . . . He constantly makes the movements of infinity, but he does this with such correctness and assurance that he constantly gets the finite out of it.[14]

Now I think that is a philosophical model for this inclusive mysticism which von Hügel is talking about. The phrase 'movements of infinity' is perhaps unusual for English ears but corresponds to something like what is meant by 'detachment' in more catholic teaching. Interestingly, von Hügel also talked about 'detachment' in a more secular context when he talked about the scientific temperament. Von Hügel felt that the scientific temperament required the same disinterestedness and detachment as the mystical quest. This brings the scientist closer to the inclusive mystic. Both of them are doing what Kierkegaard called 'looking for the infinite in and through the finite'.

Perhaps I can give a personal example of this. In my last parish it was my privilege to minister to a retired master printer. He had been brought up in the printing trade long before the advent of computers and photocopiers and had the old printer's eye for the beauty of a typeface and the setting of a page of print. He also made models – beautiful model boats and engines of infinite complexity. And he confessed to me that this was his way to God. His wife used to complain, jokingly, that he spent far too long in his workshop – but I knew (and I think she did) that he was there suspended between heaven and earth. When he died I ministered to him and he complained to me that people wanted to make him read religious books in preparation for heaven. I sensed that he had, in the stillness of his workshop, been there already, and said that he shouldn't be tempted to read religious books but should go to heaven as a printer and at that he wept copiously for a long time. To my mind he was the inclusive mystic, the Knight of Faith who lives in the finite but every instant makes the movements of infinity.

Von Hügel enlarges on his conception of the inclusive mystic by talking about love. He says that the exclusive mystic is so clear that the infinite has to replace the finite that he supposes that religion has nothing to do with politics, for example. But von Hügel pleads that personal identity is not secured by opting out of science or society but by continual purification of our engagement in the world. So the exclusive mystic opts for the love of God only where God is 'not loved perfectly until he is loved alone'. Von Hügel pleads that we should follow what he calls 'a second more difficult and rarer conception', where 'God is placed not alongside creatures but behind them, as the light which shines through a crystal and lends it whatever lustre it may have ... He is loved here, not apart from but through and in them.'[15] This is very reminiscent of many of the quotations of mystical experience given above where the light of God appears to shine from deep within the creation. Thus von Hügel reaffirms that the mystic loves the creation, just as Kierkegaard's Knight of Faith takes delight in it. He loves the creation and also through it loves God.

Thomas Merton picks up a great deal of this and reinterprets it within the mainstream tradition of catholic spirituality. The interesting thing about Merton's view of mysticism is that it underwent an enormous transformation during his lifetime. In his younger days as a monk he was set upon the traditional post-Reformation track of catholic spirituality whereby the mystical way was an ascent to God for the professed contemplative. He was embarked upon what von Hügel would have called the 'exclusive' mystical way. The crowning achievement of that period of Merton's life was his study of St John of the Cross which he called, fittingly enough, *The Ascent to Truth*.[16] He writes there in very exclusivist terms –

> First of all the contemplative life demands detachment from the senses . . . Essentially, mystical experience is a vivid conscious participation of our soul and of its faculties in the life, knowledge and love of God himself . . . God is not loved perfectly until he is loved alone.

And we know from Merton's writings that he thought that such experiences were not available to the ordinary lay person living outside of the cloister, which only goes to demonstrate how potentially élitist the 'exclusive' type of mysticism really is.

But then later in his life Merton moves to an explicitly inclusivist view. In a book about prayer called *New Seeds of Contemplation*, he writes – and the difference is palpable –

> Detachment from things does not mean setting up a contradiction between things and God – as if God were another 'thing' and as if his creatures were his rivals. We do not detach ourselves from things in order to attach ourselves to God, but rather we become detached from ourselves in order to see and use all things in and for God.[17]

Merton goes on to say that this is an entirely new perspective which many sincerely moral and ascetic minds fail utterly to see. 'There is no evil in anything created by God, nor can anything of his become an obstacle to our union with him.' Much of this shift in Merton's thought is recorded by his biographers and commentators. It is remarked upon by Merton himself in the opening chapter of *The Sign of Jonas*,[18] the journal of his middle years in the monastery. There he says that after having written that study of St John of the Cross, *The Ascent to Truth*, he moved to a more intuitive and poetic awareness of God. It is interesting to speculate on just what it was that caused such a dramatic development in Merton, and his biographers write about it endlessly. My own simple view is that gradually Merton became a more integrated and happy person and naturally discovered an 'inclusive' way to God as his delight in the countryside and in his own self replaced the war that he had been waging against himself in the earlier part of his life.

I think it might be worth mentioning in passing that some of Merton's shift from exclusive mysticism in the early part of his life as a young enthusiastic Catholic to inclusive mysticism at the end of his life where he was a rebellious monk was partially caused by events in his life but was helped by his reading of the English mystics, particularly Thomas Traherne and Julian of Norwich. He was assisted, interestingly, in finding the English mystics by the English priest, Donald Allchin, who became a Canon of Canterbury and has written very movingly himself about the mystical way.

It is worth looking at one or two further aspects of Merton's exposition of inclusive mysticism which I think will help us to understand it more clearly. First, he says that the obstacle to our union with God is not 'this world' but 'the false self'. The false self is 'the tenacious need to maintain our separate, external and egotistical will. It is when we refer all things to this outward and false self that we alienate ourselves from reality and from God.' In another place, he says that what keeps us attached to our false self is illusion. 'My false and private self is the one who wants to exist outside of the reach of God's will and God's love – outside of reality and outside of life. And such a self cannot help but be an illusion.'

Sin, he says, is living as if this illusory self is reality.

Thus I use up my life in the desire for pleasures and the thirst for experiences, for power, honour, knowledge and love to clothe this false self and construct its nothingness into something objectively real. And I wind experiences around myself and cover myself with pleasures and glory like bandages in order to make myself perceptible to myself and to the world.[19]

He then moves into a very beautiful meditation upon the resurrection of Lazarus and how when coming out of the grave you have to unwind your bandages. At the resurrection Christ left the grave clothes behind and was only identified by the love of God, not by the things which he had acquired.

So for Merton the mystical way is one which becomes more and more inclusive as his spiritual life develops. More and more he sees all things as held in God and 'mysticism' as the way to enable us to see what really is the case. All this is important because it might help us to see mysticism as not so much an escape from reality – which is what it has been accused of being in the past – but as something quite different, as that which enables us to see things in God and so be free from the false self or the illusory self which we may have adopted. Mysticism is the way to truth, not an escape from the truth.

This leads us to something about the mystical way which is often missed. Mysticism is redemptive – it brings us to the truth about ourselves. It is not a means of liberating ourselves from the world; it is not an escape, but rather a means, possibly even the pre-eminent means, by which the soul is liberated from falsity, from the tissue of imaginings within which it envelops itself, and so comes to the true and risen self which has been there from the beginning.

Six centuries earlier the German mystic Meister Eckhart had said the same thing in his own way. He emphasized the redemptive character of mystical experience in a number of passages where he talks about 'mineness' – the capacity of the soul to say 'this is mine'. Even the capacity to say 'My God', in Eckhart's view, has to be stripped away before God can fill us. He says,

> If you want to have and to find complete joy and consolation in God, make sure you are naked of all created things, of all comfort from created things; for truly so long as created things console you and can console you, you will never find true consolation.[20]

And if this sounds like a return to the exclusive mysticism which we turned away from earlier in this chapter, then beware, for Eckhart also makes it very clear that the person in whom God has truly come to birth is somebody who lives in the world and delights in the world as everybody else. It is comfort from created things that is wrong. He also makes it clear that the person in whom God has come to birth acts justly towards others because the justice of God is borne in that person. A lack of active justice is a further sign of the absence of the birth of God in the soul.

There is another singular passage in Eckhart which describes the mystic living in the world and which is very reminiscent of Kierkegaard's Knight of Faith which we mentioned earlier. Eckhart says,

> When the man of the soul is in true possession of eternal bliss, then that man meets no opposition from anything. But note, you must pay heed, such people are very hard

to recognise. When others fast they eat, when others watch they sleep, when others pray they are silent – in short all their words and acts are unknown to other people, because whatever good people practice while they are on their way to eternal bliss, all that is quite foreign to such ones. They need absolutely nothing for they are in possession of the city of their true birthright.

And so the mystical way is the way of love and non-attachment, or, to use modern language, it is the way of glory and freedom. All of the passages quoted above display a sort of glorying in the world and all of them demonstrate great freedom of spirit. I believe that modern men and women can find the same glory and freedom in their own experience and that this will enable them to glimpse God. If there is a mystical holiness for modern men and women then it must be that inclusive mysticism of which Merton and others speak so strongly. For one thing the scientific conclusions of our own age will not let us deny the importance of the created world without falling into an otherworldliness which will deny or limit the need to care for the creation. Many people in the environmental movement already believe that it is this otherworldly or 'exclusivist' stance of Christianity which has caused the crisis of the environment in the first place.[21]

I find it instructive that my own ministry has taken me more along the inclusive route both in terms of what I want to say to people from the pulpit and in terms of where I actually minister. Slowly I have moved more and more away from the city and into the countryside, not because I want to escape from people but because I want my ministry to people to be fed by the given beauty of the creation. My present vicarage faces south over open countryside to where the blue-green slopes of the Mendip hills come down to the edge of the Chew Valley lake. On a clear night I can stand in my garden and count innumerable stars, picking out the pink of the Orion nebula with my field glasses. Occasionally a spotted woodpecker will visit the garden looking for food. On the lake wild-fowl gather in their hundreds. In the lanes high on Dundry hill behind my house yellowhammers flit in the hedgerows if you are patient enough to wait for them. Seeing these things brings glory and reminds me of the glory that I and all of us are. Knowing this also sets me free. Knowing the glory sets me free to share the glory with others, to visit without fear, to minister within the community with the great freedom of grace that God pours through his creation and to speak, when called upon, the word of freedom that Christ, the Word of God, utters in and through the glory.

I discover in my reading that so many contemporary mystics have found the same to be true for them, although my own claim to mystical experience is severely limited. A little-known modern mystic whose voice reinforces the way in which I find myself called to be is Annie Dillard, a young American writer. Her account of a year alone in the Appalachian countryside is essential reading for all who seek God in and through the created order rather than apart from it. At the end of her year in a passage that is very redolent of Julian of Norwich, especially the description of the hazel nut, she quotes Emerson,

'I dreamed that I floated at will in the great Ether, and I saw this world floating also not far off, but diminished to the size of an apple. Then an angel took it in his hand and brought it to me and said, "This thou must eat." And I ate the world.' All of it. All of it, intricate, speckled, gnawed, fringed, and free. . . . A sixteenth century alchemist wrote of the philosopher's stone, 'One finds it in the open country, in the village and in the town. It is in everything which God created. Maids throw it in the street. Children play with it.'[22]

What Annie Dillard means is that the traditional quest for the philosopher's stone, where the seeker believed that it was somewhere outside of normal experience, must be replaced by the view that we have already been given it, in the shape of the created world.

FOR ACTION AND REFLECTION:

• Read again the passages above describing the experience of hearing Bach's B minor Mass or walking in the lane in Shropshire. Spend some time trying to recall any of your own experiences which could fall into a similar category. Write them down and ask yourself what they meant at the time.
• Find one of the classic mystical texts from Christian tradition. I suggest the poems of St John of the Cross, one of Eckhart's German Sermons, or a contemporary religious journal such as that of Thomas Merton (*The Sign of Jonas* is best) or Annie Dillard, *Pilgrim at Tinker Creek*, and read it slowly. Why is it important?
• Is there any mysticism in the Bible?
• Is mysticism of any use?

FOUR

Social and Evangelical Holiness

A FRIEND OF mine is the Vicar of the Isle of Dogs in the east end of London. He and his congregation recently became involved in the struggle against racism in that area. A local election had elected a councillor from the British National Party and feeling against the black and Asian communities was running very high. Nick and his people worked with the local community organizations to educate and to raise the consciousness of people about what was happening to them. This involved the wearing of rainbow coloured ribbons to indicate that people of all colours were part of God's creation and were intended to live together in harmony. Nick wrote about his experiences in his Christmas letter to his friends telling of the difficulties and of his feeling of joy when, after the next election when the British National Party candidate was rejected by the people, a shy Bangladeshi woman passed him in the street and gave him a reticent smile and a little gesture of triumph with her hand. It was a singular and moving story of faithfulness, of imaginative and creative co-operation between people of different race and religion and of co-operation between the church and local community organizations. It is a story of how principles can be put into action, not so much on their own, but rather with love and prayer and sensitivity, with attention to the needs of people and with a great deal of imagination. It was a story not without a considerable amount of pain, but also one where what we have come to call the social gospel was spoken in the life of the nation.

The story raises two important questions. The first is about holiness. Is what I have just called 'the social gospel' part of the search for holiness? Surely, people will say, holiness is to do with the personal search for God in our lives and the story about the Vicar of the Isle of Dogs, admirable though it may be, can hardly be classified as part of the search for holiness? The second question is about the witness of the Church in this area. Does the Church engage in this kind of witness as a general rule? Is that sort of witness easily found in our churches today? And if it is not then why is that the case and what does it say about our search for holy living?

The answer to these questions will become more apparent if we look back for a while at the history of the social gospel movement in the Church in this country. The witness of the Vicar of the Isle of Dogs comes at the end of a long tradition of social witness which begins back in the Victorian age with William Wilberforce. It is not always remembered that William Wilberforce, the great emancipator, whose efforts in Parliament led to the freeing of slaves and the end of the slave trade, was a committed evangelical Christian who established evangelistic and philanthropical societies, converted individuals and spread what he called 'seriousness'. He was certainly serious about the education of his children (one of whom became Bishop of

Oxford) for he gave up his seat in the Commons in order to devote himself to their education and he used to end his letters to his son, Samuel, with the word 'remember'. The Wilberforce family was, of course, a classic example of Victorian Christianity – wealthy from trade in the Baltic, deeply religious, morally serious but also reforming. Much that was wrong with both Church and State was changed by them and the source of the reform was, almost invariably, Christian principles. Wilberforce had, for example, written a tract entitled 'A Practical View of the Prevailing Religious System of the Professed Christians in the Higher and Middle Classes in the Country, contrasted with Real Christianity'. This became a sort of evangelical manifesto with its call to social morality. Nowadays, we might see much of this as rather stuffy and establishment, but then it was regarded as progressive and reforming. The main point is, however, that Wilberforce did not, indeed could not separate his sense of vocation to a holy life – what he called a 'serious' life – from his commitment to improving the social conditions of the poor. And he did this in obedience to the gospel of Jesus Christ as he understood it. For him it was the establishment of his day which had forgotten to be obedient to this gospel.

Of course, behind all of this high Victorian seriousness was the influence of John Wesley and the Methodist Movement, where evangelical piety and social concern, particularly social concern for the working man, went hand in hand. But this combination of faithfulness to God and faithfulness to social justice did not die out of the Church of England with the death of John Wesley or William Wilberforce. Much of the

best of the Anglo-Catholic Revival took a very clear
social line and I think it will be worthwhile spending
a few moments looking at one or two of those who,
in the nineteenth and early twentieth centuries, kept
the tradition of linking piety and social commitment
closely together.

There are, of course, those who are well known,
such as F. D. Maurice, Bishop Westcott and Charles
Gore. It is interesting to see that some of the issues
that Maurice and Westcott and Gore brought to the
fore are still with us, often unresolved, today. F. D.
Maurice, for example, held two Chairs at King's College, London and was a friend of Charles Kingsley,
known to us as the author of *The Water Babies*, but
known to his contemporaries as a Christian Socialist.
During his lifetime F. D. Maurice was called a 'muddy
mystic'; perhaps because of his idealized view of the
Church as the sign and sacrament of human unity.
The kingdom of Christ was quite simply the human
family, all of us. For many this was far too vague,
hence the epithet, 'muddy'. He eschewed parties in
the Church because they destroyed the unity which,
he believed, the Church should embody. The State
too was to be a sign of unity and its task was to
promote unity amongst men and women. His support
of Working Men's Colleges and his friendship with
Kingsley and other Christian Socialists was part of his
desire to see men and women united, rather than
divided by class. He also rebuked the evangelicals of
his day for their narrow, pietistic vision. He asked
them to adopt a wider vision of what the Church
could be and reproached them for their obsession with
the depravity of mankind. He sought to replace their

substitutionary atonement views with a representative one. He rejected their doctrine of hell and everlasting punishment, forfeiting both of his Chairs at King's College, London for so doing; and he rejected the evangelical doctrine of the inerrancy of Scripture. All through his theology you can trace the twin principles of love and unity which are already at work in the world. Our task, he said, is to live in ways that are consonant with what Christian theology has called the prevenient activity of God.

Maurice's mantle was taken up by B. F. Westcott who became Bishop of Durham in the late 1880s. He too was a 'muddy mystic' who supported the miners of his diocese and was President of the Christian Social Union. He too had a vision of Jesus drawing all humanity into God, and he shared F. D. Maurice's vision of unity and love with clear social consequences. He was denied the Archbishopric of York in 1890 by Lord Salisbury because of the 'socialist tendency of the speeches he has made since he became Bishop'. When Westcott died the miners of Durham attended his funeral in force and many strong men wept.

Another great nineteenth-century visionary socialist was Charles Gore, first Principal of Cuddesdon College, Oxford, and latterly Bishop of Oxford. Gore was also deeply involved in the founding of the Community of the Resurrection, a community which combined a vision of God with service to the poor and which nurtured, among many others, Archbishop Trevor Huddleston. Gore was a distinct Christian Socialist, mocked in his day not as a member of the Tory Party at prayer, but of the Socialist Party at Mass.

In 1889 Gore edited an influential and controversial book entitled *Lux Mundi*. One hundred years later, looking back on the essays it contains and the controversy it generated, it feels very similar to much of what has been said recently in the Church and makes one realize that the controversy is still largely unresolved. The Oxford University Press refused to publish *Lux Mundi*, and the eccentric Father Ignatius (who founded a monastery in the Welsh mountains with just himself and a boy) used to follow Gore around and interrupt his speeches with claims that he was not sound on the Trinity! But Gore's great contribution was not so much *Lux Mundi* as his book *The Body of Christ* which expounded the doctrine of the real presence of Christ in the Eucharist and the Church. In the Eucharist the living Christ gives himself to his people.

Maurice, Westcott and Gore were the giants of the nineteenth century who kept a spiritual theology and social action in constant creative tension. For them the search for holiness could not be separated from the pressing need to improve the conditions of poor people and working men. The point is, however, that they did not adopt these views because of some political ideology – Marxism, after all, had hardly been invented at the time – but in obedience to a theological vision of the nature of the kingdom of God. The need for personal holiness and the search for a society which cared for the poor were both part of the same vision. To suggest that they were separate issues would have simply caused these men a great deal of puzzlement. Since their time we have made personal holiness something which is quite separate from the quest for a just society. What my friend Nick in the Isle of Dogs seems to have learned is how to put these two sides of the same coin back together again. The very fact that we feel compelled to ask the question, 'What has personal holiness to do with the search for justice in society?', as we did at the beginning of this chapter, is an indication of just how far we have gone in taking for granted that these two things are disconnected.

It is worth remembering that there were a number of younger men who came under the influence of F. D. Maurice, Gore and Westcott, who never rose to the dizzy heights of being Professor of King's College twice over or Bishops of Durham or Oxford, but who laboured away in seemingly less significant places struggling to maintain the same tension in their ministry. One of these was Stewart Headlam, the founder of the Guild of St Matthew, who died in 1924. Headlam was very influenced by F. D. Maurice as a young man and revered him to the end. Two of the aims of the Guild of St Matthew were: 'to promote frequent and reverent worship in the Holy Communion' and 'to promote the study of social and political questions in the light of the Incarnation'. The Guild believed in the Church as the divine society which united believers to Christ. It also believed in the unity and brotherhood – and I am sure if they had been alive today they would have said sisterhood – of all humankind.

What is instructive for us about Headlam is the way he scorned humanists and secularists just as much as he scorned the establishment and its reliance upon class distinction. Headlam claimed that no socialist was really worth his salt unless he was also a Christian.

To be a true socialist you had to be a Christian, just as true Christians had to be socialists. Naturally he clashed with the bishops both over theology (they delayed his ordination because of the influence of F. D. Maurice on his thinking) and over his social concerns. Headlam had become Honorary Secretary of the Stage Guild, but the bishops considered the stage and especially the ballet to be the cause of terrible harm to young men. The short skirts worn by ballet girls were regarded as indecent. Because of his support for the theatre Headlam was banned from functioning as a priest.

There were a number of others who stood in the same tradition. Among them was Conrad Noel, the Vicar of Thaxted, who hung the red flag in his church and encouraged maypole dancing. There was also a priest in Somerset, Charles Marson, who was Vicar of Hambridge. Like Headlam, Marson was suspected of 'Ritual Disorders' (probably things like wearing vestments) and was visited by a member of the Ritual Commission to see what he was up to. The inspector was sent away with a flea in his ear, being told that the real disorders of the Church were the low wages paid to rural workers and the insanitary conditions in which they were allowed to live!

All of these younger, lesser, figures were deeply influenced by the earlier giants, Maurice, Westcott and Gore. They all held that catholic theology, especially a catholic theology of the Church and the Eucharist, inevitably led to a form of socialism. They also held that socialism without a sacramental catholic faith was useless secularism. They were devout, prayerful, worshipful men who served their parishes well when they were allowed to, well protected by the security of their benefices, and who worked to improve the access of the poor to the things of God.

In the twentieth century this tradition is continued in the work of a small number of priests many of whom work amongst the homeless or those suffering from the effects of HIV and AIDS. Amongst them is Kenneth Leech, one-time historian of the Catholic Socialist Movement. Leech founded the Jubilee Movement which has developed a network of groups for discussion and action and supported the publication of a number of papers, in particular the volume called *Essays Catholic and Radical* issued in 1983, edited by Kenneth Leech and Rowan Williams.[1] This volume celebrated the 150th Anniversary of the beginning of the Oxford Movement and it combines a concern for social holiness with a concern for personal and prayerful holiness before God.

But it should not be thought that social commitment is the preserve of the Anglo-Catholic wing of the Church of England. The evangelical wing has an equally distinguished history in this regard. We have already mentioned Wilberforce. Shaftesbury is the next Victorian evangelical who comes to mind. The Salvation Army and the Church Army are the two great evangelical organizations which still remain committed to the cause of the poor, the Church Army being at the forefront of some notable experiments in Christian community living amongst the poor in some of our great cities. There is also of course the YMCA and the YWCA and a number of other evangelical social movements for social holiness.

By this time we should have been able to discern

something of the answer to the first of the questions with which we began this chapter. The quest for social justice is part of the quest for personal holiness because the theological vision of these great men – from Wilberforce through to Kenneth Leech – is that the kingdom of God is concerned with wholeness of life. Personal awareness of salvation is intrinsically related to the salvation of society. In their mind there was no separation. The separation has occurred since. This has been the case in both the catholic and the evangelical wings of the Church of England. In *Essays Catholic and Radical*, Kenneth Leech and Rowan Williams say that the Jubilee movement came into being for a number of reasons, including a concern for the resurrection of the unity of contemplation and politics and a concern for the state of the Christian left with its lack of clear theological thought. They also comment that recent years have seen a retreat towards preoccupations of a mainly ecclesiastical nature. Leech and Williams also point out that whereas there was something of a resurgence in Roman Catholic social teaching under Pope Paul VI and Pope John XXIII in the shape of a number of socially orientated encyclicals, namely *Populorum Progressio*, *Pacem in Terris*, and *Mater et Magistra*, nonetheless there has been a similar retreat within the Roman Catholic Church itself in recent years from that socially committed catholicism promoted by Pope John XXIII.

Meanwhile, in the evangelical tradition a similar conclusion is drawn by David Gillett, the Principal of Trinity College, an evangelical college for the training of clergy in the Church of England. He points out that, for evangelicals, social action is never divorced from the urge to evangelize, but

> When the Church began to see this dual calling as divisible into the two separate concerns of social action and evangelism, evangelicalism showed a distinct and at times theologically defended preference for evangelism over social action – except in the overseas mission field where the two remained largely united.[2]

So it seems that across the board there has been a retreat from the creative tension between catholic or evangelical theology and social commitment. The reasons for this and the difference in approach between evangelicals and catholics on this issue should not be hard to see. Gillett places his finger on the nub of the issue when he says that the central point of evangelical spirituality is the inner conversion of the soul to God. Catholic spiritualities on the other hand centre upon the incarnation of Christ and see the Church, into which the individual is incorporated, as the continuation of the incarnation. Gillett says,

> In Catholic spiritualities the reality of the Church has an existence above and beyond the sum total of the individuals who make up its membership at any one time. It is clear that any spirituality that sees either the creation of the universe or the creation of the Church as a fundamental starting point will have a discernibly different feel from the traditional evangelical approach. One envisages the broad process of the work of God into which the individual is incorporated. The other begins with the individual when he or she responds to the work of

God's grace and thus becomes a member of the community of faith.

My concern is to point out that while it is true, as David Gillett says, that evangelicals have tended to neglect the social consequences of their faith because of their central emphasis upon the interior moment of conversion, thus lapsing into a subjective and individualistic faith, it is equally true that the catholic wing of the Church, because of its concern with 'the Church' as the source of life, has become preoccupied with liturgical or ecclesiastical niceties. And all of this has extinguished the great social commitment which was part of the rich piety exhibited by such giants of the Anglo-Catholic Movement as Father Groser of the East End or the priests in whose shoes I stood when I was the vicar of a church in North London. These men not only led pious and prayerful lives focused on the Eucharist but also set up soup kitchens and poor houses for the workers of Highgate Wood and insisted that no pew rents be levied (thus establishing a 'Free Church') so that the poor could attend the Mass just as easily as the rich.

The realization that this tradition of linking the quest for personal holiness with social action was so strong in the nineteenth century should also prompt us to ask the second question with which I began this chapter, 'Where has all this gone?' 'Why is it not widespread in our churches and what does this mean for the search for holiness?' One answer is that it has quite simply migrated. It has gone to the Third World.

We can see how this has happened if we look at one

particular social issue, that of land. The early Christian socialists in this country were very concerned about the ownership of land and the distribution of wealth. One of the earliest of them, Thomas Hancock, said in 1888, 'No English priest can hold an ideal Harvest Festival until all English land really belongs to England.' He advocated a form of nationalization of land so that the common people owned their own birthright. When we hear things like that we are inevitably reminded of the claims of Third-World liberation theologians in Latin America and elsewhere today. In Latin America, catholic theologians applied sacramental catholic teaching to a particularly entrenched social situation which had resulted in the appropriation of land by wealthy landowners. There was, and continues to be, an explosion of thought and a theological movement known now as 'liberation theology'. Much of this movement has transformed the churches, particularly in Latin America, from subservient, pious communities preserving the peace, to vibrant, sacrificial and active groups prominent in the search for social reform. Many of their educational techniques – known as 'conscientization' – have been adopted in the more developed world with no little success. The difficulty with the 'liberation theology' which resulted was that it appeared to many outside commentators, including the Vatican, to be under the influence of Marxist or Communist thinking.

I believe such criticisms to be totally wide of the mark. Liberation theology is not primarily a political philosophy but a biblical theology. This is because it is first and foremost an attempt to trace the action of God in the Hebrew Scriptures and the New Testament. The conclusion it reaches is that this action is liberating. The Children of Israel are set free from Egypt and brought into the Promised Land by God. The action of God in Jesus is to set individuals free from illness and 'possession'. Jesus himself then embodies this in the freedom of the resurrection where he is set free from the power of death.

The Eucharist of the Church is similarly interpreted by liberation theologians as the place where the believer is released from 'the powers' of darkness and so, in turn, participates in the action of God by enabling others to be liberated. This is a genuinely biblical response to a particular situation where the Christian community becomes the text and represents or repeats the action of God in its own life. The action of God is primarily seen to be that of liberation, and consequently holiness is participation in community in the liberating activity of God.

One of these Third-World liberation theologians, Jon Sobrino, also makes the point that much of the struggle of the people of El Salvador (the country where Oscar Romero was Archbishop and was murdered as he said Mass) is not just a participation in the text of Scripture but also a participation in the priesthood of Christ. By suffering and dying the people open the way to God. And so liberation theology is not only biblical but also essentially experiential in that it is a theology that makes sense of the suffering of oppressed people and interprets that experience for them in terms of the passion of Jesus.

So liberation theology is a genuine attempt to give ordinary people a spirituality which is both scriptural and experiential in terms of the life which they live.

Meanwhile here in this country or in Western Europe in general we find very little of this sort of thing. By comparison theology here has become polarized, losing its contact either with a deep and genuine striving for holiness on the one hand or a deep and genuine concern for the poor on the other. We risk captivity to the anaemia of the age.

But this is not the end of the story. While it is true that much authentic striving for a social and evangelical holiness has migrated to the Third World, some of the elements that characterized the tradition of Maurice and Gore, which we looked at earlier in this chapter, have not transplanted easily. The fragmentation in that tradition – the split between prayer and action – which we observed in this country has also followed its children overseas. This is particularly true of that part of catholic socialism which was described earlier as a 'muddy mysticism' and to my mind it is precisely that phrase which holds the key.

Liberation theology has found it extremely difficult to free itself from its rationalist and European origins. It is not always a 'home grown' product. Much liberation theology although written in the Third World sprang up in response to the work of European theologians like Moltmann and Pannenburg. In 1965 Moltmann wrote a *Theology of Hope* which was extremely influential at one point upon a whole generation of Third-World theologians.[3] So much liberation theology is an intellectual transplant and as such it risks bypassing the actual experience of the poor, particularly of poor women, since intellectual theology in the Third World is still the preserve of men.

This was borne out for me recently when I attended

a conference on liberation theology in Andalucia attended by a number of Spanish and Latin American liberationists. It was a conference where the practice denied the content of the talks given. The lectures, all about the importance of liberation, were all given by men and each lasted for more than an hour and a half. The women found it extremely difficult to participate. When some of us Northern Europeans awoke from sleep or boredom and raised this issue, we were accused of neo-colonialism!

Further evidence for the 'masculine' and rationalistic nature of much liberationism is found in the fact that it relies heavily upon a philosophy of action. God is the active one. He acts to liberate his people. I am quite sure that this disregards the substantial nature of the incarnation, reducing that mystery to a mere activity on the part of God. God's identification with human nature or subsuming of human nature into himself must be seen as real. Its effect is to bring about salvation not just by imitation on our part together with the subsequent reliance upon the human will that this entails, but by transformation. Salvation comes not through imitation of the action of God but through faith that human nature has actually been taken into God in Christ. 'He became as we are so that we might become as he is.' This mystical idea of grace perfecting and fulfilling nature is actually much more in accord with the scriptural understanding of salvation than the energetic but deeply tiring view that we must continually keep up with what God is doing. It is not a question of imitating God but of opening the self to God's action.

There is, however, one Third-World theologian

whose work does espouse this 'muddy mysticism'. He is an Orthodox theologian from India, Paul Verghese. Verghese is one of the few Third-World thinkers who has tried to grapple with the whole question of what freedom really means. He searches the Orthodox tradition for a theology of liberation and traces some of the difficulties we have experienced so far in trying to understand liberation theology to an over-reliance on St Augustine. He points out that Augustine spoke about two kinds of freedom, what he called *libertas major* and *libertas minor*. One is freedom to choose between good and evil, the other freedom from sin in the bosom of God. We moderns would call one the 'right', rather than the freedom, to choose and the other the 'right' to freedom from constraint. We would value both of them extremely highly as the basis for a civilized society of individuals.

Verghese is staunchly unconvinced and believes both of these freedoms, or 'rights' as they have become in Western society, to be inadequate. His view is that we need to develop a much richer understanding of freedom. For him the essence of freedom is creativity. 'The essence of freedom lies in spiritual creativity, in being the originator of a causal chain.' Most liberation theologians leave the impression that they are concerned with liberation in the senses favoured by Augustine – freedom to choose and be emancipated from internal or external constraint. They encourage the view that freedom is an end to be achieved rather than a beginning – a state of being rather than the condition for growth.

Verghese expands his view as he reflects on the work of the fourth-century Greek theologian, Gregory of Nyssa. Gregory's view was that freedom is basic to God and consequently to humankind made in the image of God. Humanity shares in God's nature. This freedom has a number of elements, among which are spontaneity and boldness.

> A clear conscience and the presence of the Spirit make it possible for us to turn boldly and spontaneously towards God and to enter his presence. This free access to God belongs to the original image and the regaining of it is part of man's liberation. To join the heavenly choir, to sing and to dance without worry and anxiety, to rejoice and again to rejoice, this is true liberty.[4]

Verghese points out that freedom from bondage is still only within the negative phase of freedom. This is necessary but it is only a prelude to the discovery of a more positive and creative freedom based upon the free worship of the free God by people originally created free who long to regain their freedom in God. 'The march of freedom', he says, 'is ceaseless, for it is the march toward the being of him who created the world in freedom, who dwells in unapproachable light, who is Freedom . . .' And so this Orthodox theologian points to worship, prayer and the ethical life – the love of God and the service of humanity – as being the proper place for the discovery of creative and positive freedom. Other freedoms are necessary, but not enough. He says, 'Freedom is more than liberation . . . Liberation only places us on the threshold of freedom . . .'

I would like to build on this evaluation and say that the problem that I have with liberation theology is that it is ultimately intellectual and conceptual and so reductionist in its outlook – it relies upon a reduced or limited understanding of human beings as, ultimately, intellectual and conceptualizing beings. It also places action rather than transformation at the centre of its understanding both of God and humanity. It is not mystical enough. For when it comes to the question of the creation and transmission of freedom, reasoned arguments will not suffice. It is in the end a matter of looking for the divine in human beings, and awareness of our divinity is not conveyed merely by language or arguments or by concepts or by persuasion to do certain things. We need to become aware of the presence of God within ourselves and allow that to give us our freedom. We still need the 'muddy mysticism' of F. D. Maurice and his followers.

Of course, the question then arises as to whether we can find any examples in the modern world of this 'muddy mysticism' being the source of a holiness in the service of the poor. Is such a combination possible or are we left with nothing more than an exhausted tradition in Western Europe and an intellectualized struggle in the Third World? Looking around it appears that there are two individuals in modern times who have struggled through to the sort of position which Paul Verghese begins to sketch out in his thinking about freedom. Neither of them achieved this without a struggle nor without being challenged, either by others or by the situation in which they placed themselves. One is Thomas Merton at the end of his life and the other is a lesser known Trappist from the last century who thought his contribution would die with him, Charles de Foucauld.

Merton's journey to a mystically based socially committed holiness came to fruition through a very testy and difficult correspondence with Rosemary Radford Reuther, the American feminist theologian. Rosemary Reuther entered into correspondence with Merton in the late 1960s and accused him of ignoring the importance of action and of sitting on his backside in the monastery instead of coming out into the world 'where the real demons are'. Merton replied that monastic life has a lot of demons of its own but it also 'can play a very helpful part in the worldly struggle precisely because of the different perspective which it has and should preserve'. He said that the monastic life is not a striving for perfection but a realization of identity. This was one of the conclusions I came to earlier in this book when looking at monastic spirituality and the contribution of the Desert Fathers. The monastic life, Merton claimed, reduces you to the condition of being a human being and nothing else. This is something which everyone can realize wherever they are. This condition of being 'merely human' is the resolution of all alienation and the preparation for a real return into the world without masks and without defences. 'This is a proper contribution', Merton said, 'to the quest for freedom in the world.' He claimed that the greater freedom was the inner one and it is that which will make the stronger political contribution in the long run. In other words, he talks about inner creativity and how this is shared in the common life, whether of the monastery or of society, not transmitted by argument. What is plain to anybody reading the exchange of letters between Merton and Rosemary Reuther is that Merton was caught on the

hop by the ferocity of the onslaught from this formida-
ble woman opponent and forced to think through
what he thought about the contribution which the
monastic life could make to the struggle for freedom.[5]
Until then he had had the field to himself; but
Merton's stubborn insistence on the need for an ill-
defined 'something else' in the face of the neutralizing
effect of corruption and political fakery on all political
action, however well motivated, remains valid and
could be held even more strongly today in the light of
all that has happened in the political world since he
wrote. In many ways he has turned out to be the more
politically realistic of the two, but at that time he
looked, and felt, like a naive outsider. We must be
glad that he was challenged but also glad that he did
not capitulate.

The French soldier turned monk turned hermit,
Charles de Foucauld, had no feisty woman theologian
with whom to grapple in the desert. He had to
struggle with his aristocratic upbringing and the colo-
nial and missionary ambitions of his native country.
All of those he transformed into good before he was
tragically killed. De Foucauld was a wealthy French
officer who, after a dramatic conversion experience,
left the army and gave himself to the monastic life,
eventually living as a hermit in the Sahara amongst
the Tuareg. De Foucauld lived a life of intense discipline and silence. In the end he was killed but many
years later his life and writings sparked the founda-
tion of a number of religious communities, generally
known as the Little Brothers or Little Sisters of Jesus.
They live with the poorest of the poor and they work
and spend much time in contemplative prayer. They

try to combine holiness of living with social commitment, totally. They do not preach, but attempt, in Charles de Foucauld's phrase, to 'cry the gospel with their lives'. Yet their influence is liberating. There is the true story of one of the Little Brothers of Jesus who lived in a prison in Africa as a simple way of sharing his life with the poor. One night he overheard the other prisoners arguing about who he was and why he was there. There were various answers. Some said that he was a spy sent by the authorities. Some said he was mad. Then one person said, 'He's here to keep the rumour of God alive.' This is a deeply costly way of preserving the tension between faith, theology and social commitment. It is not one which relies upon the intellectual arguments of some liberation theologians but is, none the less, liberating. It is liberating because of its mystical commitment to God and its mystical commitment to the people. De Foucauld says,

> In order to be a leaven of hope, bury yourselves away silently. Seek no efficacity but that of giving a little more joy and a little more love to those around you. When someone meets you he may discover that God loves him and that he is unique in the world.[6]

The work of the Little Brothers and Sisters is also, unintentionally, a political statement. It combines faith with social commitment. They live fraternally in small groups, devoted to prayer, work and friendship for their fellow workers and so they make a clear statement which is both theological and political by what they are rather than by what they do. They live a

protest against suffering and death, against the oppres-
sion of poverty, against exploitation. But they live
this protest by loving those with whom they live and
work. One Little Brother of Jesus living in São Paulo
writes this:

> In a situation of injustice and oppression . . . there have
> been days when I've asked myself whether following
> Jesus of Nazareth was any use or whether it would be
> better for us to get into the struggle more directly. But I
> think that this life of imitating Jesus of Nazareth is a
> part of the direct struggle. To live a quality of love for
> the poor people whom we have made our friends, that
> indicates who God's friends are and where true riches
> lie. That lets loose the subversive power of the gospel.
> It strikes at the psychological roots of the situation of
> oppression, a perverted way of thinking that finds it
> normal that the well-furbished fellow be respected and
> admired and a poor fellow be disregarded. These psycho-
> logical structures are false and our lives have to announce
> that God doesn't see things that way. It's like the
> brothers said when we were together for our Chapter –
> the witness of friendship is already a path of evangelisa-
> tion and a ferment of liberation, for simply looking with
> love and sensitivity at a poor person, at a person rejected
> by others, provokes a liberating interior transformation
> and contains a manifestation of God's love. And besides,
> this loving look given to someone poor is a testimony
> to others, for it reveals the greatness and dignity of
> those who are considered little and poor.

That is a very moving statement of the type of social
and evangelical holiness which I believe is appropriate

to our day. One could duplicate it time and again from the letters of the Little Brothers. It implies an understanding of the gospel which provokes interior transformation – and so is truly evangelical – but results in a social transformation, which you may not see. It is rooted not in doctrine, but in friendship – the place where God begins to show his face.

In a sense it is like the witness of Jesus with the woman taken in adultery. When they brought the woman to him he did nothing, but wrote in the sand. He does not actively condemn the action of the woman, nor does he begin to campaign for the changing of the Mosaic code which brought her there, ready to be stoned for her adultery. He makes no political statement, but writes in the sand. The poet Seamus Heaney, commenting on this, says,

> The drawing of these characters in the sand is like poetry, a break with the usual life, but not an absconding from it. It does not say to the accusing crowd or to the helpless accused, now a solution will take place. It does not propose to be instrumental or effective.[7]

The point being, of course, that while a solution was not proposed a solution none the less took place. And I would want to add that probably more has happened in Christian history because of that silent writing in the sand than might have happened as a result of any of the political campaigns which Jesus might have fought in his day. More change has been wrought in more social structures and in more political lives by Jesus' loving, forgiving, accepting silence.

The twentieth century has, then, seen a number of

valiant attempts at social and evangelical holiness. My purpose in this chapter has been to show that these attempts are the direct heirs of the Victorian tradition of social holiness which began with Wilberforce and was continued in Maurice, Westcott and Gore among others. The difficulty has been that in the twentieth century this tradition has fragmented. It has fragmented in two ways: one, in that the link between personal and social holiness is no longer seen to be intrinsic; and second, in that the tradition has, by and large, migrated to the Third World. But even there the fragmentation has pursued its practitioners, leaving the liberation theology movement in a very aetiolated and intellectualized condition.

I then traced the attempts of a number of people to repair this tradition of linking personal and social holiness. Paul Verghese is the theologian who shows how the fragmentation has ocurred because of the influence of St Augustine and wants those who talk about freedom to return to the more integrated vision of Gregory of Nyssa. Meanwhile figures like Thomas Merton in his later life and Charles de Foucauld in his desert fastness, had to struggle with very different challenges but these struggles forced them to bring these two strands back together again and so overcome the fragmentation to which they were heirs.

I have not asked my friend, the Vicar of the Isle of Dogs, what it was that enabled him to link the quest for personal holiness and social action. Maybe it was the challenge he faced in an urban wilderness. We must simply be thankful that here and there, in the face of powerful contemporary forces which lead to fragmentation, the old unity is being restored.

Rediscovering Holiness

- Find a group of Little Brothers or Sisters of Jesus and ask them to come to your church or your study group and talk about what they do.
- Join them for prayer if you can.
- Find a Christian group in the inner city – the Church Army has some – and ask them what they are doing and why.
- Is God always on the side of the poor? Look through Scripture to find out.
- The Epistle of James links personal and social holiness very clearly. Why, then, did Luther call it an 'Epistle of straw'?

Epilogue

So WHERE HAVE we come? Have we discovered how run-of-the-mill Christians living in the complexities of the modern world can aspire to holiness? What is holiness for modern people?

On the surface this book has searched for holiness by surveying some of the contemporary movements for renewal in the Church. It has ranged extremely widely. We have seen evidence of the resurgence of monastic or quasi-monastic life in Europe. We have looked at the wealth of contemporary biblical interpretation and asked whether there can be an authentic renewal of biblical patterns of living. We then reviewed the surge of interest there has been in mysticism and at what has happened to the fine tradition of social and evangelical holiness which was part of the English Church in the nineteenth century. I asked how it might be possible to rediscover that tradition today.

Inevitably the overall approach has been somewhat objective in style. We have looked at church life from a more speculative and, indeed, intellectual point of view, seeing what has happened as phenomena within the Church. At this level certain conclusions can be drawn. For example the resurgence of the monastic ideal and of interest in St Benedict can only be seen as a distinct gift to the Church. But our study also led us to say that it is distinctly questionable whether 'community life' in itself guarantees that search for integrity and wholeness before God which the monastic way essentially embodies. We found ourselves looking beyond Benedict (who was, of course, a genius and left us the parochial pattern with his emphasis on 'place' and stability) to the Desert Fathers and their search for the true self in Christ. In their day this was often hidden behind the formal 'false' self of the institutional church which was, as Thomas Merton says, 'fabricated under social compulsion in the world'. A renewal of monasticism in our day which does not see that this inner liberation is its central goal is not sufficient to face the situation in which we are placed and would do no more than replicate, within its communal or monastic life, the ills of the world in which that community is set.

I came to a similar set of conclusions when I turned to the current rediscovery of biblical spirituality. Once again, although there is massive evidence, particularly in evangelical and charismatic circles, of a rediscovery of the Bible, there is much that is questionable. What is needed is an abandonment of fundamentalism together with certain types of liberalism in order to allow ourselves actually to live the text of Scripture in a deeply symbolic way and to discover its living truth within ourselves. Much of the work done by feminist biblical scholars, many of them Roman Catholics, will point us more surely in that direction as will the work of those who seek archetypal patterns within the text. In talking about the resurgence of interest in mysticism we saw that this resurgence was only valid if it was – borrowing a distinction from von Hügel – an inclusive rather than an exclusive mysticism. This mysticism is the way of love for God through all things rather than apart from all things. Our study of the nineteenth and twentieth-century movements for social holiness once again lead us to posit this 'only if'. This time it was an 'only if' about the nature of freedom – freedom is not simply political freedom, although that is an essential step. Freedom is also creativity, and creativity implies the willingness and capacity to accept what I called a 'muddy mysticism' as being at the root of all action which seeks to establish God's kingdom in this world. Otherwise this action will either be absorbed into 'politics' or be reduced to mere theatre.

This means that each time we have looked at the resurgence of the quest for holiness in our day, whether it be monastic or mystical or biblical or social, we have found a genuine resurgence to welcome – but always with an 'only if'. The serious problem which the Church faces is how to welcome these holiness movements without neglecting the 'only if' and so ensuring that the movements are not simply a form of fundamentalism in a new guise. This problem faces all of the churches, of whatever denomination. It is also a problem which much of the movement towards holiness itself has not been willing to address. But unless it is addressed then the Church will not become a more holy Church, simply a more emotional and fragmented one.

Although we have looked at this resurgence as a corporate phenomenon in the Church it is always individuals who are involved in it. Individual and personal faith is very much at a crisis point in the contemporary world. It desperately needs the renewal which the movements we have described provide, but once again only if this renewal is appropriated in an interior and existential manner along with the normal exterior practice of 'church life' with all that entails, otherwise the renewal will only affect those who have time for it or who can afford it. Merely joining a new community or rediscovering the Bible or pretending to mysticism and contemplative prayer or rushing off to protest about the debt crisis in itself profiteth me nothing. All of these have to be accompanied by a deep interior conversion, a divesting of the false self and a realization of the presence of the hidden Christ in the deepest part of the self AND a discovery of the same Christ hidden within the Church and in the created order. All of that must, in its turn, be held within a movement of repentance and renewal. As Rilke says, 'You must change your life', but all of it must be changed. Once again the contemporary resurgence of interest in holiness has not always taken itself seriously enough and so has been left with the superficial, the fashionable and the experimental.

Furthermore this survey has also brought to light a number of clues to the essence of holiness which are not as eyecatching as the obvious signs of renewal we have been looking at. In spite of them being less obvious these clues are none the less essential. The current emphases in the contemporary quest tend to overlook their importance. The first of these is the invisible or secret nature of holiness. I have already referred to this at a number of points. I said that holiness was not 'self-regarding' – indeed it is essential for real holiness that it almost does not know itself. Holiness that continually thinks about itself and how holy it really is has totally lost its way. This is illustrated by the story about a book on the spiritual life which dealt at length with the virtue of humility. Apparently the book had gone out of print and the author approached the publisher and said that it was high time that the book was re-printed, because it was far and away the best thing on the subject! We do well to remember Meister Eckhart's 'man of the soul' who is in possession of eternal bliss. 'But note,' says Eckhart, 'You must pay heed. Such people are very hard to recognize. When others fast, they eat . . .'

It is significant that this picture of the unknown holy one is not just a Christian one. It also occurs in other faiths, most notably in Buddhism where those who have reached Nirvana do not enter it, but return to the world for the sake of those who are still on the way. In a series of paintings of the progress of the soul in Zen Buddhism, the last picture of the series shows the enlightened one returning to the market place with open hands. He or she is there 'in the world' but there 'simply', there 'for others', without fuss or exhibition.

Those on the road to holiness within the Christian tradition need to recall the words of Jesus in the Sermon on the Mount, where he says:

> Beware of practising your piety before others in order to be seen by them . . . when you give alms do not let your left hand know what your right hand is doing, so that your alms may be done in secret – and your Father who sees in secret will reward you . . . Whenever you pray, go into your room and shut the door and pray to your Father who is in secret. (Matthew 6.14 NRSV)

It should also be remembered that this emphasis on the invisible or secret nature of holiness is *not* a call for something esoteric or unusual – i.e. having a secret, private or special way to God which only the initiated or the better informed or the spiritually practised know about. There is a real danger that the emphasis which currently exists on 'spiritual training' will encourage a form of spiritual élitism which is a long way from the intention of Jesus. Much New Age spirituality is no more than a form of spiritual élitism for those who can afford it. As one clergyman said to me when looking at a programme for a New Age retreat, 'Ah, not the higher consciousness but the higher selfishness!'

It is, rather, a humble and ordinary way to God that I am talking about which does not advertise itself and which goes about its good work quietly and by unknown paths. I remember in my last parish there was a very famous occasion when at a very large church council meeting one enthusiastic student stood up and berated the congregation for not being vigorous or spirit-filled or whatever it was that we were supposed to be. I remember one woman stood up, absolutely furious. She said, 'You do not know! You do not know!' And she was quite right, of course, because the poor student did not know what people were doing, quietly, secretly; visiting the sick, working in quiet unknown ways, not advertising themselves, not standing up and waving their hands.

This emphasis upon what you might call the secret or invisible aspect of holiness is vastly encouraging because quite apart from anything else it opens the doors of holiness to the 'ordinary' person who is striving in quiet ways on their own. We have to look there – to the little people of this world – just as much, if not more so, as to the spiritually famous.

Just as there is a secret or invisible aspect to holiness, so also this secret or invisible nature of holiness is found in the midst of everything else. It is not something which only occurs when you take yourself away from life, it is something which 'breaks through' at any point in daily life and which undergirds daily life. Holiness, or its presence in life, is sacramental – it is hidden in and through reality and in and through everything we do. A holy one is not somebody who has extracted themselves from living. He or she is rather someone who has discovered the interior dimension of all that happens to them and of all that is. Sacramental Christian holiness says that God is to be found in and through our activity in this world, in the midst of all that is and all that he has made. Love is all you need. 'Love all God's creation, the whole of it and every grain of sand in it. Love every leaf, every ray of God's light. Love the animals, love the plants, love everything. If you love everything, you will perceive the divine mystery in things.'[1]

We should remember the Little Brother of Jesus whom we quoted in an earlier chapter who said that living a quality of love for the poor people whom we have made our friends indicates who God's friends are and where true riches lie. He went on to say that simply looking with love and sensitivity at a poor person actually provokes a liberating interior transformation and contains a manifestation of God's love.[2]

The third essential factor which this quest for holiness has revealed is the necessity of living from the inner centre – from that point of inner integration from which love springs. St Teresa of Avila speaks of this inner centre when she says:

> This secret union (the spiritual marriage of the soul with God) takes place in the deepest centre of the soul which must be where God himself dwells and I do not think there is any need of a door by which to enter it . . . all that has been described [so far] seems to have come through the medium of the senses and faculties . . . but what passes in the union of the spiritual marriage is very different. The Lord appears in the centre of the soul . . . just as he appeared to the Apostles without entering through the door when he said to them, 'Pax Vobis' 'Peace Be With You'.[3]

This image of Christ entering into the innermost part of the soul without hindrance, just as Christ entered into the room where the apostles were gathered after the resurrection without coming through the door, is central to the quest. It is mirrored in all of the other mystic writers. Meister Eckhart talks of God the Word being birthed in the soul. Julian of Norwich says, 'Greatly ought we to rejoice that God dwells in our soul; and more greatly ought we to rejoice that our soul dwells in God. Our soul is created to be God's dwelling place, and the dwelling of our soul is God, who is uncreated.'[4]

The insight of the Christian mystical tradition is that there is a point, a place, at the very deepest level of our beings which is not riddled with division and conflict, but is a place made ready in us for the Word of God. Division and conflict in our lives result from a lack of relationship with this divine centre. Deep within the self there is a place for unity with God which, in the end, even sin cannot reach.

This divine centre – the room with no door, to use Teresa's language – has received different names in Christian history. Eckhart's term is 'ground' – the term which Tillich took up in this century when he talked of the ground of our being. Merton adopts it and calls it the hidden ground of love. My own view is that this 'ground', this room with no door, exists within everybody and everybody is capable of accessing it in different ways, from the highest to the lowest. The master printer whom I referred to in chapter three did it in his model workshop. The trouble is that it is hidden from us. We have lost touch with this inner ground and so the holy life is distanced from us. I think that socially we seem to have lost touch with it because of our emphasis upon getting and spending. Our moral life has been poisoned. The causes of this loss are manifold. We have alienated ourselves from it by a combination of fear and the desire to achieve. Once we can reunite ourselves with this inner ground then we will rediscover the reality of God's unceasing presence, and prayer and action will arise from us like a great fountain of love and the holy life will begin.

Let me dwell for a moment upon this quest for the mysterious inner centre described by Teresa as the room with no door into which Christ, the risen one, enters freely. This mysterious inner centre is also described by the psychologist Carl Gustav Jung. Jung talks about 'the integrative centre' in a number of places – he also gives this centre a deeply religious dimension. He says, 'I cannot define for you what

God is. I can only say that my work has proved empirically that the pattern of God exists in every man, and that this pattern has at its disposal the greatest of all energies for transformation and transfiguration of his natural being.'[5]

Psychotherapists in the Jungian tradition do their best, in dealing with human souls, to unite their patients with this mysterious integrative centre and so be healed. But it is not just Jung who describes it, it is also the poet. Seamus Heaney, a contemporary Irish poet, speaks of it several times in his book, *The Government of the Tongue*. He comments there on the writing of Osip Mandelstam, the dissident Jewish Russian poet who was murdered by Stalin. 'Mandelstam', he says

> implied that it was the poet's responsibility to allow poems to form in language inside him, the way crystals formed in a chemical solution. He was the vessel of language. His responsibility was to sound rather than to the state . . . . Mandelstam wanted to give himself over to his creative processes without the interference of his own self-censorship or the imposition of a Soviet orthodoxy . . . for him, obedience to poetic impulse was obedience to conscience; lyric action constituted radical witness.[6]

Later on, Heaney says the same thing in stronger words while talking about another poem by another poet:

The lines are inhabited by certain profoundly true tones, which, as Robert Frost put it, 'were before words were, living in the cave of the mouth'. They do what poetry most essentially does, they fortify our inclination to credit promptings of our intuitive being. They help us to say in the first recesses of ourselves, in the shyest, pre-social part of our nature, 'Yes. I know something like that too. Yes, that's right. Thank you for putting words on it'. ... A poet then becomes an antenna capturing the voices of the world, a medium expressing his own subconscious and the collective subconscious.

In other words the poet too is somebody who, if they are to be loyal to their calling, must be in contact with 'the cave of the mouth', they must own and rely upon their mysterious inner centre, the room with no door, the first recess of themself, the shyest pre-social part of our nature, and allow it to speak. Once we do that, once we own that centre, then, I believe, we become believers; not immediately orthodox believers, that will come if we place ourselves in the right context, but believers none the less. We will have opened the door to the transcendent within our beings.

From an acknowledgement of this divine centre, a number of things should begin to happen. First, true social action rather than mere politics becomes possible and necessary, because the justice of God within you is released. A moral imperative is activated within the soul. Second, true prayer is also released because prayer is the language of the room with no door. Prayer as primary speech flows from that inner place. Third, true biblical living becomes possible because it is at the level of the collective Christian unconscious, deep within the soul that we meet the biblical people.

At this level we can rejoin the people of God. But here too, finally, we meet Christ, the Word of God.

You may have already been wondering, if you have followed this book closely, what has happened to Jesus. He has only been mentioned once or twice. That is because he is at the centre of things. Jesus is the Word who is spoken by God from all time, at the centre of all things and in our centre. Holiness of living is not so much a matter of imitating Jesus but of allowing him to be spoken in the centre of our being, of acknowledging and owning that he is spoken in our centre and that he works his work of grace there, redeeming us from our illusions. He is the one who owns the room with no door.

So the search for holiness is essentially allied to the search for integration, the search for our hidden centre, who is Christ. When we ally ourselves to him there, then holiness of living becomes possible. But this is a gift, something which happens by grace not by works. It is also a shock, a reversal of values, a stripping of the old, a conversion, what theologians call an ascesis. In order to re-find our true selves an ascesis, a stripping of our inordinate ego, has to take place. We have to go, if not into the desert then into its modern equivalent so that we may know what is real and discover the existence of the room with no door. This ascesis or stripping can be undertaken voluntarily – we may go into the desert – or it may come upon us.

I wrote earlier in this book of a recent TV programme which interviewed people who had been kept hostage for considerable periods of time. The producer had thought that many of them would be broken, but not so. One came home to mend his marriage, another put his business in order, another returned to the Church. All lived more simply now and with more peace. The TV producer said he could have reproduced this many times. These people were given, unwillingly of course, an ascesis, a terrible stripping, which actually had the effect, the shocking and unexpected effect, of re-uniting them with their true selves. When Brian Keenan was freed from his long captivity he expressed some of this by saying, 'I feel like a cross between Humpty Dumpty and Rip van Winkle. I have fallen off the wall and suddenly awake I find all the pieces of me before me. There are more parts than I began with . . .'[7] This is a very significant remark and contains a very significant clue to the nature of holiness in the modern world. He found more of himself. I believe that we must come through an ascesis of our inordinate desires to be in touch with the 'more parts' of ourselves because this will enable us to share in the work of God within us.

Sometimes this ascesis will happen in the most amazing circumstances – as it did for Brian Keenan. It also happened in the most amazing circumstances for Etty Hillesum, the Jewish woman who went voluntarily to Auschwitz from Holland during the war. Her diaries record her discovery of God deep within her. She wrote, 'That part of myself, that deepest and richest part in which I repose, is what I call "God"'. Then movingly, she begins to speak – and she wrote this in one of the transit camps – of those whom she meets, each of them potential houses with empty rooms where God may also come and repose as he does in her.

There they are, bundles of human misery, desperate and unable to face life. And that's where my task begins. It is not enough simply to proclaim you, God, to commend you to the hearts of others. One must also clear the path towards you in them, God . . . Sometimes they seem to me like houses with open doors . . . and every one must be turned into a dwelling dedicated to you, oh God. . . . There are so many empty houses, and I shall prepare them all for you, the most honoured lodger.[8]

Etty Hillesum wrote those words in the middle of the most terrible deprivation this century has known. She was a Jew in the war on the way to her own death after the sudden death of the man she had loved beyond all others. There is no doubt that she had been moving towards such a position before he died, but also it seems, little doubt that the ascesis of his death finally released that compassion in her. So it happened to her.

What, then, can we say in conclusion? There can be little doubt that the holy life is under considerable pressure in the modern world. Many of the strategies which have been developed over the past two decades and which are outlined in the preceding pages are, undoubtedly, a form of response to that pressure and so are to be broadly welcomed. The difficulty is that they are often no more than part of the way we live now and consequently unable to speak to the modern world with the prophetic quality which holy lives should display. Religion risks becoming part of the package which any well-shod Westerner possesses in addition to everything else. We should not think that because somebody has allied themselves to one or other of the holiness movements of our day, these things in themselves will bring about holy living. I vividly remember reading a magazine in a dentist's waiting room one day which had a supplement on healthy living. After all the usual items such as diet, exercise, stress management and the like, there came a section devoted to religion. Had the seeker after healthy living also been on retreat lately? A list of suitable houses was appended. Even prayer can become an item on the consumerist shopping list. That is why the secret, humble and ordinary ways to God are even more necessary than before. These ways are not part of the culture of our day and will enable us to speak to it from deep within.

In a consumerist age the journey is harder than we think. We need to be ready to be stripped, like Brian Keenan or Etty Hillesum, and be ready in our nakedness to discover the secret point of encounter with God. We need to be ready to receive and then to defend, at a point beyond all our own desirings, the life of God within us. The discovery is primary – for it will restore and refresh us in these days when effort and achievement is all-conquering. But the defence is equally important, for in this world the main danger that besets us is forgetfulness. We are surrounded in our contemporary consumerist society by the modern waters of Lethe, the classical river of forgetfulness. If we continue to plunge into them we shall preserve our false selves, surround ourselves with bandages, even religious ones, but forget who we are. Holiness is remembering who you really are.

Notes

PROLOGUE

1. Herbert McCabe, *God Matters* (Geoffrey Chapman, 1987).
2. R. S. Thomas, *Counterpoint* (Bloodaxe Books, 1990).

CHAPTER ONE

1. Alasdair MacIntyre, *After Virtue* (Duckworth, 1981).
2. David K. Gillett, *Trust and Obey* (Darton, Longman and Todd, 1993).
3. John Cassian, *Conferences*, tr. Colm Luibheid (The Classics of Western Spirituality, Paulist Press, 1985).
4. Esther de Waal, *Seeking God* (Collins/Fount, 1984).
5. There are numerous translations of the Rule of St Benedict. I have used that of David Parry, *Households of God* (Darton, Longman and Todd, 1980).
6. There are several good translations of the *Verba Seniorum*, the best is by Benedicta Ward, *The Sayings of the Desert Fathers* (Cistercian Publications, 1975).
7. Simon Tugwell, *Ways of Imperfection* (Darton, Longman and Todd, 1984).
8. Thomas Merton, *The Wisdom of the Desert* (Sheldon Press, 1974).

CHAPTER TWO

1. *Independent*, 1 February 1993.
2. Robin Lane Fox, *The Unauthorised Version* (Viking, 1991).

Notes

3. Henri Boulad, *All is Grace – God and the Mystery of Time* (SCM Press, 1991).
4. Timothy Radcliffe, 'Time and Telling – How to Read Biblical Stories' (*New Blackfriars*, March 1991).
5. James Alison, *Knowing Jesus* (SPCK, 1993).
6. Sandra M. Schneiders, *The Revelatory Text* (HarperCollins, 1991).
7. William Shannon, *Seeking the Face of God* (Collins/Fount, 1988).
8. Walter Brueggemann, *The Bible and Postmodern Imagination* (SCM Press, 1993).
9. Melvyn Matthews, *The Hidden Word* (Darton, Longman and Todd, 1993).

CHAPTER THREE

1. *We Believe in God* (Church House Publishing, 1987).
2. Alister Hardy, *The Spiritual Nature of Man* (Oxford University Press, 1979).
3. The best book about this is Michael Mayne, *This Sunrise of Wonder* (Collins/Fount, 1995).
4. A number of these experiences are quoted in John V. Taylor, *The Christlike God* (SCM Press, 1992).
5. William Wordsworth, 'Ode: Intimations of Immortality from Recollections of Early Childhood'.
6. Cited by Anthony Storr, *The School of Genius* (André Deutsch, 1988).
7. See his encounter with an orange in his account of his captivity in Lebanon – Brian Keenan, *An Evil Cradling* (Hutchinson, 1992).
8. Thomas Traherne, *Selected Writings* (Carcanet, 1980).
9. Edwin Muir, *Collected Poems* (Faber and Faber, 1960).
10. Thomas Merton, *Conjectures of a Guilty Bystander* (Sheldon, 1977).
11. William H. Shannon, *Silent Lamp* (SCM Press, 1993).
12. In a book review cited by John V. Taylor in *The Christlike God* (SCM Press, 1992).

Notes

13. Rowan Williams, 'Butler's Western Mysticism: Towards an Assessment', *Downside Review*, 1984, cited by Nicholas Lash, *Easter in Ordinary* (SCM Press, 1988).

14. Søren Kierkegaard, *Fear and Trembling* (Princeton University Press, 1941).

15. Friedrich von Hügel, cited by Nicholas Lash, *Easter in Ordinary* (SCM Press, 1988).

16. Thomas Merton, *The Ascent to Truth* (Burns & Oates, 1962).

17. Thomas Merton, *New Seeds of Contemplation* (Burns & Oates, 1962).

18. Thomas Merton, *The Sign of Jonas* (Hollis and Carter, 1953).

19. These extracts are from *New Seeds of Contemplation*.

20. Meister Eckhart, *The Essential Sermons*, tr. E. Colledge and B. McGinn (The Classics of Western Spirituality, Paulist Press, 1981).

21. For an interesting look at this problem see Ian Bradley, *God is Green* (Darton, Longman and Todd, 1990).

22. Annie Dillard, *Pilgrim at Tinker Creek* (Harper and Row, 1974).

CHAPTER FOUR

1. Kenneth Leech and Rowan Williams (eds.), *Essays Catholic and Radical* (Bowerdean Press, 1983).

2. David K. Gillett, *Trust and Obey* (Darton, Longman and Todd, 1993).

3. English translation 1967, SCM Press.

4. Paul Verghese, *The Joy of Freedom: Eastern Worship and Modern Man* (Lutterworth, 1967).

5. See Thomas Merton, *The Hidden Ground of Love*, letters selected and edited by William H. Shannon (Farrar, Straus & Giroux, 1985).

6. The Little Brothers and Little Sisters of Jesus, *Cry the Gospel with your Life* (Dimension Books, undated).

Notes

7. Seamus Heaney, *The Government of the Tongue* (Faber and Faber, 1988).

EPILOGUE

1. Fyodor Dostoevsky, *The Brothers Karamazov*, cited by Michael Mayne, *This Sunrise of Wonder* (Collins/Fount, 1995). His whole book is very instructive in this regard.

2. Little Brothers and Little Sisters of Jesus, *Cry the Gospel with your Life*.

3. Teresa of Avila, *The Interior Castle*, Seventh Mansion, tr. Allison Pears (Sheed and Ward, 1946).

4. Julian of Norwich, *Showings*, trans. Edmund Colledge and James Walsh (Classics of Western Spirituality, Paulist Press, 1978).

5. C. G. Jung in a letter to Laurens van der Post, cited in van der Post, *Jung and the Story of Our Time* (Penguin, 1978).

6. Seamus Heaney, *The Government of the Tongue* (Faber and Faber, 1988).

7. Brian Keenan, *An Evil Cradling* (Hutchinson, 1992).

8. Etty Hillesum, *An Interrupted Life* (Washington Square Press, 1985).

Further Reading

In addition to the books quoted in the text and referred to in the notes the following will be found helpful:

GENERAL
Donald Nicholl, *Holiness*. Darton, Longman & Todd 1981.
Ann and Barry Ulanov, *Primary Speech*. SCM Press 1985.
Cheslyn Jones, ed., *The Study of Spirituality*. SPCK 1986.
Christian Spirituality. 3 vols in World Spirituality series. SCM Press 1985.
Melvyn Matthews, *God's Space in You*. Hunt and Thorpe 1992.

ON MONASTICISM
Thomas Merton, *The Monastic Journey*. Sheldon Press 1977.
Jean Leclercq, *The Love of Learning and the Desire for God*. SPCK 1978.

ON SCRIPTURE
Melvyn Matthews, *The Hidden Word*. Darton, Longman & Todd 1993.
John Eaton, *The Contemplative Face of Old Testament Wisdom*. SCM Press 1989.
Robert Alter, *The World of Biblical Literature*. SPCK 1992.

ON MYSTICISM
Olivier Clement, *The Roots of Christian Mysticism*. New City 1993.

Further Reading

Bernard McGinn, *The Foundations of Mysticism*. SCM Press
1991.

ON SOCIAL HOLINESS
Kenneth Leech, *The Eye of the Storm*. Darton, Longman &
Todd 1994.